D1547564

Seeds of Illness, Seeds of Recovery

Illustrated with richly detailed clinical vignettes, *Seeds of Illness, Seeds of Recovery* offers a fascinating investigation into the origins, modes and treatment of psychical suffering.

Antonino Ferro provides a clear account of his conception of the way the mind works, his interpretation of the analytic understanding of psychopathology, his reconceptualization of the therapeutic process, and implications for analytic technique derived from his view of the therapeutic action of psychoanalysis. Drawing on and developing the ideas of Wilfred Bion, Ferro gives a unique perspective on subjects including:

- Container inadequacy and violent emotions
- The waking dream and narrations
- 'Evidence': starting again from Bion
- Self-analysis and gradients of functioning in the analyst

This highly original approach to the problem of therapeutic factors in psychoanalysis will be of interest to all practising and training psychoanalysts and psychotherapists.

Antonino Ferro is Full Member of the Italian Psychoanalytical Association and the International Psychoanalytical Association. He is a child and adolescent psychoanalyst and is especially concerned with adults with serious pathologies.

THE NEW LIBRARY OF PSYCHOANALYSIS
General Editor   Dana Birksted-Breen

The New Library of Psychoanalysis was launched in 1987 in association with the Institute of Psycho-Analysis, London. It took over from the International Psychoanalytical Library, which published many of the early translations of the works of Freud and the writings of most of the leading British and Continental psychoanalysts.

The purpose of the New Library of Psychoanalysis is to facilitate a greater and more widespread appreciation of psychoanalysis and to provide a forum for increasing mutual understanding between psychoanalysts and those working in other disciplines such as the social sciences, medicine, philosophy, history, linguistics, literature and the arts. It aims to represent different trends both in British psychoanalysis and in psychoanalysis generally. The New Library of Psychoanalysis is well placed to make available to the English-speaking world psychoanalytic writings from other European countries and to increase the interchange of ideas between British and American psychoanalysts.

The Institute, together with the British Psycho-Analytical Society, runs a low-fee psychoanalytic clinic, organizes lectures and scientific events concerned with psychoanalysis and publishes the *International Journal of Psycho-Analysis*. It also runs the only UK training course in psychoanalysis which leads to membership of the International Psychoanalytical Association – the body which preserves internationally agreed standards of training, of professional entry, and of professional ethics and practice for psychoanalysis as initiated and developed by Sigmund Freud. Distinguished members of the Institute have included Michael Balint, Wilfred Bion, Ronald Fairbairn, Anna Freud, Ernest Jones, Melanie Klein, John Rickman and Donald Winnicott.

Previous General Editors include David Tuckett, Elizabeth Spillius and Susan Budd. Previous and current Members of the Advisory Board include Christopher Bollas, Ronald Britton, Catalina Bronstein, Donald Campbell, Sara Flanders, Stephen Grosz, John Keene, Eglé Laufer, Juliet Mitchell, Michael Parsons, Rosine Jozef Perelberg, Richard Rusbridger, Mary Target, David Taylor.

ALSO IN THIS SERIES

THE NEW LIBRARY OF PSYCHOANALYSIS

General Editor: Dana Birksted–Breen

Seeds of Illness, Seeds of Recovery

The Genesis of Suffering and the Role of Psychoanalysis

Antonino Ferro

Translated by Philip Slotkin

The translation of this work has been part-funded by SEPS
Segretariato Europeo per le Pubblicazioni Scientifiche

Via Val d'Aposa 7 – 40123 Bologna – Italy
tel +39 051 271992 – fax +39 051 265983
seps@alma.unibo.it – www.seps.it

Brunner-Routledge
Taylor & Francis Group

HOVE AND NEW YORK

First published in Italian as *Fattori di malattia, fattori di guarigione* by
Raffaello Cortina Editore, Milan, 2002

First published in the English language 2005 by Brunner-Routledge
27 Church Road, Hove, East Sussex, BN3 2FA

Simultaneously published in the USA and Canada
by Brunner-Routledge
270 Madison Avenue, New York, NY 10016

Brunner-Routledge is an imprint of the Taylor and Francis Group

Typeset in Great Britain by RefineCatch Ltd, Bungay, Suffolk
Printed and bound in Great Britain by TJ International Ltd, Padstow, Cornwall
Paperback cover design by Sandra Heath

This publication has been produced with paper manufactured to strict environmental standards
and with pulp derived from sustainable forests.

British Library Cataloguing in Publication Data
A catalogue record for this book is available from the British Library

Library of Congress Cataloging-in-Publication Data
Ferro, Antonino, 1947–
[Fattori di malattia, fattori di guarigione. English]
Seeds of illness and seeds of recovery: the genesis of suffering and the role of psychoanalysis /
Antonino Ferro [translated by Philip Slotkin].
p. cm. – (The new library of psychoanalysis)
Translation of: Fattori di malattia, fattori di guarigione. Milano: Cortina, 2002.
Includes bibliographical references and index.
1. Psychoanalysis. 2. Suffering. I. Title. II. Series.

RC506.F423 2004
150.19′5–dc22
2004007583

ISBN 1–58391–828–0 (hbk)
ISBN 1–58391–829–9 (pbk)

Contents

Contents

Foreword

Thomas Ogden

This is a book of narratives – narratives constituting thinking and dreaming, narratives conveying the analysand's unconscious commentary on the analyst's interpretations, narratives mediating the self-analytic work of the analyst, to name only a few. This introduction represents still another narrative: my own effort to schematically map out what I believe to be the central themes of this book. These are themes that reappear in every chapter, but do so in a way that does not feel repetitive because each new appearance of these topics involves Antonino Ferro's reapproaching them from a different vantage point. This process generates a sense of an ongoing thinking process that yields ever more textured conceptions of the analytic enterprise.

The movement of the ideas in this book that I will track entails a progression from first, Ferro's conception of the way the mind works to second, his reconfiguration of the analytic understanding of psychopathology (which he derives from his model of the mind) to third, his reconceptualization of the therapeutic process, and finally to some implications for analytic technique that are derived from his view of the therapeutic action of psychoanalysis.

I would like to emphasize that just as Ferro is creating his own Bion for the purposes of developing his own thinking, I am creating my own Ferro in what follows. This introduction will have succeeded if it is of use to the reader in creating his or her own reading of and use of Ferro's work.

A model of the mind

I will begin this narrative with an effort to convey a tentative sense of the meanings of some of the words that will be used. These 'definitions' are merely starting places inasmuch as the words accrue ever-changing meanings as they are used in this introduction and in the book as a whole. Bion invented intentionally meaningless terms in order to escape the 'penumbra of associations' (1962a, p. 2) that the existing analytic terminology has taken on. He uses the term 'Beta elements' to refer to the most rudimentary impressions that experience makes on the mind. They are raw sensory (emotional) data, the most vague and inarticulate registrations of emotional states such as anxiety, fear, terror and dread. Beta elements have the feel of 'undigested facts' (Bion's favourite metaphors for psychic functioning are derived from the workings of the digestive system). Beta elements cannot be linked in the process of generating thoughts or stored as memory. They are fit only for evacuation, for example, by means of projective identification, addictive behaviour or violent acting out.

'Alpha function' is Bion's term for an unknown set of mental operations by which β elements (raw impressions of emotional experience) are transformed into α elements. It is here that Ferro's contributions come strongly into play. He conceives of α elements as 'emotional pictograms' (p. 56). 'The α element is the proto-visual (or proto-auditory, etc.) component of thought' (p. 1), but not itself a thought. Its 'existence shows that what was exerting pressure in β form has been transformed into a *visual pictogram* [that carries the emotional force and valence of the β elements from which they are derived, e.g. feelings of hate, envy, jealousy, terror, infantile adoration, omnipotent grandiosity, and so on]' (p. 1).

Ferro compares individual α elements (individual pictograms) to the individual, unorganized shots that a camera operator may take in the course of a day of filming (Ferro's favourite set of metaphors is drawn from cinematography). These pictograms (which may be thought of as a small segment of a camera operator's developed film) are organized by the director into sequences that are 'viewable'. Ferro terms these sequences of α elements 'narrative derivatives'. Thus, in agreement with Bion on this matter, Ferro conceives of two stages or 'loci' of mental activity: the operation of α function and the creation of narrative derivatives (e.g. dreams, free associations, poems, thoughtful reflection and so on) as opposed to operational thinking.

Ferro elegantly elaborates on Bion's (1962b, p. 306) conception of a mental 'apparatus for thinking'. In addition to the work of α function and the creation of pictograms (α elements) from raw emotional impressions (β elements), there is a 'second level', 'an α meta-function' of mental functioning – 'the apparatus for thinking thoughts' (p. 52) that makes use of available α elements for the creation of 'narrative derivatives'. These narrative derivatives – 'a syncretic narrative mosaic of emotionally salient facts' (p. 52) – constitute not only thoughts, but also the thinking of thoughts in a way that can be used in self-reflection and for purposes of conscious and unconscious psychological work.

The second form of α meta-function introduced by Ferro is the 'apparatus for dreaming dreams' (p. 52). The narrative capacity, the ability of the mind to generate genuine thinking and dreaming, involves the workings of the interplay of the dialectics involving the psychological tensions generated between the paranoid schizoid and the depressive positions, between the container and the contained, and between tolerated doubt and the selected fact. (All of these attributes of thinking and dreaming hold in common the capacity to sustain a growth-promoting interaction between the need, on the one hand, for coherence and, on the other, an equally strong need to release oneself from the security and potential stagnation of closure in the interest of generating new possibilities. Ferro is careful to caution against the valorization of the narrative capacity. The moment-to-moment work of the metaphorical camera operator (α function) producing pictograms (α elements) is no less creative than the work of the director (the narrative capacity) who assembles the film clips (the pictograms) into creative linear and non-linear narratives.

A reconfiguration of the analytic conception of psychopathology

On the basis of his notion of the two levels or 'loci' of psychological functioning (the workings of α function and the apparatuses for thinking and dreaming), Ferro proposes that we conceive of psychopathology as taking three forms: one having to do with absent or impaired α function, a second involving a dysfunction of the apparatuses for thinking and dreaming, and a third associated with trauma – an influx of β elements that exceeds the capacity of α function to process them.

The psychopathology involving failure of α function results in a psychological situation in which the mind is devoid of visual pictograms (α elements) with which to create narrative derivatives. Hence the apparatus for thinking and dreaming has nothing to work with. Under such circumstances the individual may not have been able to form a mind. In the second category of psychopathology, the individual is able to generate α elements, but lacks apparatuses for thinking and dreaming. Consequently, the person cannot do anything with the available α elements.

The third form of psychopathology proposed by Ferro is the outcome of trauma – the quantity of raw emotional stimulation (β elements) exceeds the individual's capacity to transform β elements into potentially thinkable form (α elements). Beta elements are evacuated by such means as excessive projective identification, violent or perverse acting out, and a splitting off and projecting of the fear of the unprocessed emotional experience into another person (for example, into members of a racial minority who are viewed as dangerous, repellent and inferior).

A reconceptualization of the therapeutic process

Ferro's conception of how psychoanalysis works is derived from his conception of the way the mind works. Ferro, like Bion, is far less interested in exploring the specific configurations of unconscious fantasy (e.g. the Oedipus complex and the infant's envious attacks on the insides of the mother's body) for this work, they believe, has already been done successfully by Freud and Klein; rather, Ferro's focus is on how we succeed and how we fail to psychologically process our emotional experience:

> I am concerned here mainly with the qualities the other's [e.g. the analyst's] mind must have: the capacity to receive, to leave in abeyance, to metabolize, to return the elaborated product to the subject and, in particular, to 'transmit the method'. This is achieved by returning the product in unsaturated form and allowing the subject's [e.g. the analysand's] mind as it were to learn its trade in the workshop of the other's.
>
> (p. 16)

'To transmit the method' – this lies at the core of Ferro's view of the therapeutic action of psychoanalysis. If patients can be helped to develop an apparatus for thinking (as well as α function), they will be in a position to process their emotional experience on their own.

Ferro elaborates on this idea later in the volume:

> The analyst . . . presents him- or herself as a person capable of listening, understanding, grasping and describing the emotions of the field and as a catalyst of further transformations – on the basis that there is not *an unconscious to be revealed*, but a capacity for thinking to be developed, and that the development of the capacity for thinking allows closer and closer contact with previously non-negotiable areas. In more radical terms, the analyst does not decode the unconscious but brings about a development of the conscious mind and the gradual broadening of the unconscious, in accordance with Bion's conception . . . of psychoanalysis as a probe that broadens the field it is exploring.
>
> (p. 102)*

Implications for technique

In the course of this volume, Ferro offers a great many beautifully rendered, richly detailed clinical vignettes. It is principally in living with Ferro in various analytic situations created in his writing and in the experience of reading that

---

* I have quoted Ferro at length here in part because his fine writing contains almost no extra words and is therefore very difficult to paraphrase.

the reader learns about Ferro's analytic technique. More accurately, the reader finds that he or she has been transformed by the experience of reading these clinical accounts and that he or she no longer listens to or lives emotional experiences with patients in quite the same way as he or she had previously.

Nonetheless there are two principles of technique suggested by Ferro that I would like to mention. First, in keeping with the notion of the dream-quality of the analytic session, the analyst is often best served by reversing the conventional dictum that it is best to think before you speak; Ferro suggests that it is very frequently more productive for analysts to speak before they think and then to listen to themselves so as to engage their own unconscious life and that of the analytic field generated by patient and analyst (p. 9).

Second, for Ferro, it is essential to attend to what the patient says (verbally and non-verbally, consciously and unconsciously) after the analyst makes an interpretation, not only as a reflection of the make-up of the patient's unconscious internal object world, but as a 'real-time' (p. 107) commentary on the analyst's interpretation.

Bion once said to an analyst who was consulting with him on her analytic work, 'The way *I* do analysis is of no importance to anybody excepting myself, but it may give you some idea on how *you* do analysis, and that *is* important' (Bion 1978, p. 206). Ferro amply succeeds in this volume in realizing this vision of psychoanalytic teaching and writing.

References

Bion, W.R. (1962a) *Learning from Experience*, New York: Basic Books.
—— (1962b) 'A theory of thinking', *International Journal of Psychoanalysis*, 43: 306–310.
—— (1978) 'São Paulo clinical seminars', in *Clinical Seminars and Four Papers*, F. Bion (ed.), Abingdon: Fleetwood Press, 1987.

1

SEEDS OF ILLNESS AND THE ROLE OF DEFENCES

As an approach to the problem of the therapeutic factors in psychoanalysis, it seems to me helpful to consider first the seeds of illness and the defences deployed by patients.

We may accept the view of Bion (e.g. 1962, 1963, 1965) that every mind, at birth, needs another mind in order to develop. This development takes place through an interplay of projections and introjections. Primitive anxieties and sense impressions are evacuated into the mother's mind (by projective identification) and, after 'processing and decontamination' by the maternal α function, returned to the child in the form of representable elements (α elements) together with the method for processing them (the α function).

The child's primitive projection of evacuated anxieties and sense impressions calls for a process of reception, transformation and return that includes the 'instructions' for developing the 'unknown factor' capable of changing β into α elements. In the normal course of this process, which is repeated over and over again, the α function gradually becomes operational in the child's mind.

From then on, and to an increasing extent in 'non-emergency' situations, the system operates as follows: proto-emotions and proto-sense impressions – i.e. β elements – are transformed by the child's α function into α elements through the correct functioning of this introjected unknown (the α function).

The α element is the proto-visual (or proto-auditory, etc.) component of thought; its existence shows that what was exerting pressure in β form has been transformed into a *visual pictogram* (Rocha Barros 2000). For instance, the first pictographic reflection of a primal experience of rage and revenge might be 'a blood-filled swimming pool'.

Alpha elements are formed constantly and constitute the building blocks of waking dream thought – that is, of the proto-visual matrix that constantly 'films' sensations and sense impressions, turning them into images that cannot be directly known.

The proto-visual film (a sequence of α elements) produced in this way by the α function must undergo further operations in order to attain the status of thought and narrative image, and hence of internal or shareable discourse.

The 'narrative derivatives' (Ferro 1998a, 1998b, 1998c, 1999e, 1999f, 2001b) of this waking dream thought act as 'carriers' towards the knowable by means of operations whereby a narrative fabric is woven. These operations are bound up with the development of ♀ and of ♂, and the possibilities extend from narrative unravelling (Ps) to clear-cut woven structures (D) and the interplay of 'negative capability' and the 'selected fact'.

This second level entails the sufficient development (which is always consequent upon a good enough relationship) of more elaborate mental qualities, such as that of ♀ through repeated experiences of micro-being in unison, or of ♂ which discovers possible ways of existing if it encounters an elastic and available ♀. It also entails the development of 'negative capability' and the ability to withstand Ps (mediated by the experience of the emotions present in the other's mind), and of the 'selected fact' and of D – i.e. the capacity to mourn – which always takes place by way of the encounter with the capacity to mourn (the presence of the third party) in the other's mind.

Two loci of pathology can readily be distinguished on the basis of this simplified schema: (a) severe pathology in which the α function is lacking, and (b) pathology due to maldevelopment of ♀♂, Ps↔D and/or NC↔SF (i.e. container/contained; paranoid-schizoid position/depressive position; negative capability/selected fact).

All type (a) pathologies involve a primal deficiency in the formation of the visual pictogram, in which the 'mind' itself may even have failed to form. This situation may be likened to a cine camera with no film stock: the basic frames out of which the eventual movie should be composed are lacking. In type (b) pathologies, on the other hand, 'α elements' *are* formed, but the apparatus for processing them is deficient. The film is exposed, but then either it is not developed (there are no 'narrative derivatives') or the directorial function required to edit the vast number of frames shot – the Ps↔D work – is lacking, or else there is no place to keep the developed film (absence of ♂♀), and so on.

However, besides type (a) and type (b) pathologies, there is another possibility. Here the quantity of sensory stimulation, whether exteroceptive or proprioceptive, outstrips the capacity of the α function to form α elements. We then have a 'traumatic' situation, in which the quantitative level of stimulation (β elements) exceeds what can be transformed into α and rendered thinkable. This may be referred to as type (c) pathology, due to accumulation and trauma, in which trauma is occasioned by any situation that gives rise to more β than can be transformed into α and then processed and woven into emotions and thoughts.

There are of course an infinite number of possible combinations of (a), (b) and (c).

In an excess situation of type (c), in which there are more β elements than can be metabolized, various defence mechanisms may be deployed to cope with them. (It is obviously not easy to distinguish between an excess of β and a deficiency of the α function or of Ps↔D, ♀ ♂ or NC↔SF.)

The first defence mechanism is the formation of *undigested facts* (partially processed β elements stored in 'lumps') waiting to be transformed by an α function: I have termed these 'balpha' elements (Ferro 1996a, 1999a), and they are bound up with the transference.

We are familiar with other defence mechanisms – for example, splitting (in which the amount of β that cannot be processed is split off and projected); disavowal; negation; psychosomatic disorders; hallucinations; characteropathic acting out; perversions; psychic dismantling; or narcissism.

I am discussing defence mechanisms and the resulting symptoms together for the sake of simplicity; they could also be classified by severity, time of onset and ease of transformation.

Take, for example, 'narcissism'. This is a successful defence mechanism that operates when there is no 'place' to weave and elaborate proto-emotional states, which are then split off, projected and caused to be experienced by others, who are treated in spite of themselves as subsidiary α functions. The hard core of 'narcissism' coincides with an agglomerate of compacted balpha elements.

As stated, the common element in all defences is that they allow an excess of β elements to be managed in normal or catastrophic situations. (Let me say in passing that, as a species, we constantly face an excess of β elements and that, on the social level too, we devise strategies to evacuate, split off, hyper-control or phobicize the quantities of proto-emotions and proto-sense impressions that we are unable to transform into 'poetry of the mind' – i.e. into thoughts, emotions and affects. Wars, oppression and racism are some of these mechanisms, the investigation of which does not, in my view, fall within the competence of a psychoanalyst – for in order for there to be a specific 'analyst', there must also be a specific 'patient' and a specific 'setting', and if one of these elements is lacking, the other two cannot exist either.)

Of course, we all constantly deploy every single defence mechanism, but these defences become pathological only when they become 'established' in the place of flexible mental functioning. Whereas on the one hand they are a source of (sometimes very severe) pathology, on the other they are nevertheless a successful means of warding off even worse mental catastrophes, such as swamping of the mind, total mental dysfunction or even the complete failure of mental development.

The relevant therapeutic factors here would be 'reparative positive' elements to counterbalance the negative ones discussed above, which we can now reconsider in terms of type (a), (b) and (c) pathologies, bearing in mind that most patients are in effect chimeras of types (a), (b) and (c).

In accordance with the same scheme, there are type (c) analytic treatments, in which the patient's α function and apparatus for thinking thoughts are intact, but burdened with an excess of 'undigested facts' that give rise to transferences and projective identifications, which can be resolved only if the analyst can help in the process of assigning meaning or new meaning. These are the relatively few patients deemed analysable by classical criteria, who can tolerate classical interpretations because they have 'a place' to put them and 'means' of working them through, with the result of enrichment.

There are also type (b) analytic treatments, in which the undigested contents can be tackled only after work has been done on the mental functions that are lacking – e.g. a deficiency on the level of ♀ or of Ps↔D oscillations. These concern borderline and narcissistic pathologies in which the α function is operational but its products are unmanageable; in this case, a classical interpretation often generates more persecution than growth, because there is nowhere to accommodate it and no 'way' of using it.

Then there are type (a) analytic treatments – research analyses – in which the α function is significantly deficient, so that the β→α work must be 'redone' (or, in this case, done for the first time) by the transformation of 'discrete quanta' of β into individual α elements, so that individual α elements can be formed and the method of forming them can be introjected.

In these cases classical, or elaborate, interpretations merely constitute further sensory stimuli that give rise to evacuation, as Bion himself points out when he states that even 'thoughts' can be evacuated like β elements if the capacity to receive them is lacking (Bion 1962).

For an autistic child, a point-by-point, frame-by-frame elaboration would make more sense than a complicated and elaborate exhaustive interpretation, which would merely be an evacuation of the analyst's truth in the absence of a receiver.

I shall attempt in the following chapters to illustrate clearly the appropriate techniques for working on levels (c), (b) and (a).

In passing, I should like to make a brief comment about the 'death instinct'. It is in my view a real entity, but only in the sense of a transgenerational legacy of accumulated β elements which it has not been possible to transform and elaborate. In other words, I do not believe in a death instinct as such, but consider that there are transgenerational amounts of β elements that outstrip the present capacity of our species to elaborate them. When things go well, we call this accumulation the psychotic part of the personality which each of us shares with all mankind. In other cases, we refer to it as destruction, or the death instinct; but surely this is merely the residue over and above what it has been possible to elaborate in thought. The issue here is purely quantitative, as our capacity for mentalization still falls short of our requirements, so that the 'discarded material' remains active, exerting pressure, and often causes us to act out, commit acts of violence, or fall victim to psychosomatic or mental illness.

Another concept to be reflected upon anew, if we are to be 'in unison' with the patient, is 'omnipotence', whereby the patient, for example, exercises, or attempts to exercise, absolute control over the object. In my opinion, this style of relationship is a 'necessity' for the patient, for two main reasons.

In the first case, total control over the world and within relationships serves to minimize sensory and proto-emotional afferences where the α function is deficient (as in autistic 'control'). Here, the control avoids the genesis of potentially unmanageable proto-emotional states (precursors of emotions); the patient is like a tightrope walker inching her way along the thinnest of cords knowing that the slightest breath of wind could be fatal.

Second, jealousy and the need for possession may be concealing a 'shipwreck syndrome', in which, owing to early relational shortcomings, the subject needs the object just as a shipwrecked non-swimmer needs the plank he is clinging to.

In the first situation, the patient cannot tolerate the slightest change; she keeps everything around her, including inanimate objects, 'under control' and tyrannizes everyone so as to prevent changes that might give rise to proto-stimuli, which would be unmanageable.

In the second situation, the patient exercises possessive and jealous control out of the fear of 'sinking' or drowning if he does not 'cling' to the object. 'I'm like a flight controller,' one of these patients said, 'and if anyone wants to leave me I'll cut their legs off.'

The concept of 'frustration' also calls for clarification. Let us consider the example of a negative response to a demand. The problem is not so much the mourning thereby involved, but that 'frustration' entails a change in the subject's state of mind, with the generation of sense impressions versus proto-emotions. If the α function is insufficient, the turbulence arising cannot be managed, so that, because it cannot be 'pictographed in the form of α elements', it becomes a source of ill-being that can be relieved either by evacuation or, in favourable circumstances, through successive cycles of 'mental rumination'.

In the case of violence against the self, I also regard defences as the lesser evil. They are like a lizard that 'sheds' its tail: although mutilated, the creature saves most of itself. Splitting, for instance, is an instance of violence against the self, but the splitting off of unmanageable parts is often the only way to survive. If this is true of mutilation involving parts of the self, I believe it applies in the same way – where an appropriate capacity for mentalization is lacking – to many forms of self-mutilation and self-harm. In anorexia, for example, emotions of uncontainable violence are split off and 'starved' because this is the only possible way of managing them so as to save what can be saved.

The aim of this eulogy of defence is, of course, to understand the profound reasons for its existence. Obviously, it can only be a starting point for finding

5

other strategies to save the mind that involve less sacrifice of the self, of the internal world or of the body.

Psychic suffering often has its origins in the trauma of availability/non-availability, or, better, the gradient of availability, in the other's mind, together with the type and quality of emotions present, with which, as Bion would say, the mind of the other is suffused. If the analyst's mind is cluttered with emotions different from those expected by the patient (by virtue of the patient's pre-conception), the encounter will, because it lacks 'fulfilment', be traumatic, even if there is no actual non-availability or rejection, but only a failure of the pre-conception (expectation) to 'mesh' with the actuality (fulfilment).

Following a situation of this kind, which he described as a 'lack of interaction' and 'lack of response' (i.e. on this level the other's mind ought – mostly at least – to 'respond', and to respond in accordance with expectations), one of my patients dreamed that, while walking along a road he knew from his childhood, he could see a flood in the distance. The rising waters were not so threatening that he was in danger of being swept away, as they were far off. Perhaps some glaciers were melting. He was there with his children, whom he was protecting, but then along came a gang of 'characteropaths', who were also not particularly dangerous, and although the gang kidnapped them, there seemed to be a happy ending.

The lack of response – the failure to 'mesh' – is a wound, but seems also to be a frustration that can melt something that was previously frozen and unnarratable. Furthermore, the wound is tamponed by the characteropathic keloid. Other keloids, in my view, include erotization, excitation and narcissism.

When one of my patients, Luigi, was able to regain contact with his 'primal sense of emptiness and loneliness', he was able to relinquish the 'superabundant stoppers' he had used to close off the profound 'hole' in his being so that he could live. The superabundant stoppers had been certain harsh character traits, narcissism and a tendency to Don Juan-ism. Once the 'breach' had been found, the analysis was able to repair this ancient wound, which must have resurfaced in the transference, so that these hitherto essential defensive strategies could be dispensed with.

In most cases, the trauma with which psychoanalysis is concerned is the (often repeated) micro-trauma of the mismatch between expectation and reality: analysis allows this situation to be repeated in the presence of someone with whom the patient can 'see' and 'repair' the primal damage – which may also have affected the development of the apparatus for thinking or even the apparatus for the formation of the visual sub-units of thought itself.

This of course immediately raises the issue of the psychoanalytic model to be espoused and of the resulting theory of technique.

A change of setting had been agreed with a male patient, who thereby lost the sense of the continuity of our meetings. He began one of his sessions by telling me how he had come to blows with someone who was trying to steal his car. This patient was a seriously ill characteropath with a tendency to evacuation.

How was this communication to be seen? It could be regarded as a manifest illustration of oedipal conflictuality and interpreted as such. Another possibility was the repetition of something that could not be remembered, in which case the need would be to overcome the patient's resistances and defences so as to remove the veil of repression preventing the traumatic memory from resurfacing. On another level, it might be considered that the aim of the analysis was to make the upward-pressing unconscious fantasies conscious, thus 'detoxifying' them, so that the patient's 'rage' at the analyst, who had deprived him of something by which he set great store, could be interpreted.

Alternatively, if the priority was the patient's mental functioning and encouragement of his capacity to think (development of $\female$), the analyst could seize on the emotion of 'having been ill-treated, which had generated more emotions than he could manage'. This would acknowledge the traumatic event, the emotions generated by it, and the difficulty of metabolizing them. In this way, the analysis would remain on the level of the 'manifest text of the patient', who would then feel that his own view was shared and that he had an analyst who was relieving him of a burden instead of one who weighed him down with 'truths' about himself.

In such a situation, the analyst will of course bear in mind that intolerance of change is a sign of incapacity of the α function and of $\female \male$ to metabolize and cope with change-induced proto-emotions. From this last viewpoint, the focus will be not so much on historical or fantasy contents as on how to develop the patient's capacity for transformation and containment, through the experience of micro-being in unison.

If a female patient said: 'With the money I give you, you buy your wife designer clothes,' this remark could be heard in different ways. It could be construed as an oedipal scenario of exclusion and rage; as an alternative fantasy scenario dominated by envy of the parental couple; or, more 'simply', as a communication in which the patient is telling the analyst that she feels he is giving her 'designer interpretations' for her adult parts, which can mate with the analyst in an adult way, but that there is also a part of herself that is still excluded and alien, which she does not yet feel to be 'held'.

The same would apply if a woman patient came for her Monday session and said: 'Did we see each other on Friday?' This could be seen as a devaluation of the analyst, an 'evanescence' of the internal object, or a valuable intimation that 'we didn't see each other' on Friday – that is to say, that a real encounter did not take place.

Of course, even if we start from the aspect with the greatest relational significance in the present ('there is a part of me that feels that it is not getting anything from you; on Friday you were not able "to see me" – i.e. to allow an encounter to happen'), this must subsequently link up with the patient's fantasies and history. However, these fantasies, when 'processed and metabolized' in the here and now, will undergo transformations that will, by the process of *Nachträglichkeit*, inhabit the patient's internal world and history in a new way.

In field terms, we are concerned with what happens in the session – with narrations, narremes, proto-emotions, sense impressions and the apparatus for elaborating and managing all of these. The aim of analysis is to facilitate the development of the 'potentialities' of the patient's mind laid down in the species as pre-conceptions, which, however, require appropriate 'fulfilment' through the encounter with the other's mind.

The focus will then be on the functional or dysfunctional working of the patient's mind, the functional or dysfunctional working of the analyst's mind, and the functional or dysfunctional working of the relationship to which the encounter between the two minds gives rise – allowing development (in both patient and analyst) or causing involution (in both patient and analyst).

Once the capacity to form pictograms (visual images) and to weave them into narrative sub-units through their derivatives has been developed, attention can turn to the contents; however, this process should in most cases be only initiated by the analysis, and then be continued by the patients for themselves. The situation may be likened to the problem of washing laundry. Once there is an electricity supply (the α function) and a working washing machine (the apparatus for thinking thoughts), everything else can be done without the appliance engineer and the electrician.

The same applies to the relationship in the present. If the engineer provides us with a camera that produces ugly, inadequate photographs, there is no point in working on these poor-quality images or trying to identify the people and landscapes they depict with a view to determining how distorted they are. It would be much more sensible, as everyone would expect, to get the camera working properly instead.

Stefano

Stefano began to wonder about 'people' he kept on meeting, who, he thought, were following him. From the analytic context, it was a fairly obvious course to suggest to him that he was coming into contact with a variety of different aspects of himself and that perhaps he ought not now to be still trying to understand 'who' the analyst was in whom he had for so long deposited these aspects of himself, but should instead be wondering 'Who am I?'

There followed a dream in which the patient had three enormous baskets of plants; he had a place for two of them, but not for the third, which was different. It was easy to put it to him that he might be thinking of aspects of himself as things that could be integrated even if there was not a space for them all.

8

Next day he needed to communicate something to me urgently: for the first time he had discovered – in an underground railway carriage – that depth, height and thickness existed. Having previously lived in a totally flat world, he was now bowled over by this discovery, whereby he now saw the whole world differently, with a space, depth and three-dimensionality he had not known existed. I immediately thought of Edwin Abbott's *Flatland* (1899), a fine tale of a two-dimensional world, and told him that he seemed to have moved on from plane geometry to its three-dimensional, or 'solid', counterpart. Stefano went on to say that the many surfaces of himself could now link up with each other and acquire the dimension of thickness; previously he had always thought of himself in either one way or another, or in yet another. I told him that, now, thickness and depth belonged to him too and to his internal world – so he could think of himself as a boarding-house that could 'accommodate' the various parts of himself, including those he feared and despised most. Now he need no longer be like the two-dimensional figure in one of his dreams who beat everybody up, evacuating emotions that then came back to persecute him since he could not 'keep them inside'. All this, he opined, was due not to the analysis but to the 'drug' he had taken, even if he was afraid of appearing 'ungrateful' by saying so. I told him that the boarding-house must also contain a room for 'ungrateful' people, and that the important thing was that the 'miracle' had happened; it seemed to me immaterial which 'saint' was responsible for it.

Here, I felt that Stefano was voicing an important truth: what had helped him to emerge from Flatland was not the interpretations – the strictly analytic activity – but the 'drug' represented by all the mental operations I had performed in the sessions over the years without immediate interpretations ensuing from them, by my assumption of his anxieties and by the gradual transmission to him of the 'method of dealing with them'.

This leads me to reflect on the analyst's mental functioning in terms of all the 'non-interpretive' operations – for interpretation, whether saturated or unsaturated, is merely the last act in a series of processes of transformation and searching for meaning. When conducting supervision groups on clinical cases I increasingly find myself reversing the dictum 'think before you speak' into 'speak before you think', because one can then make contact with the dream-like functioning of the mind, which can create more connections and meanings than any 'reasoning'. After all, our task is to discover a new and original meaning in 'facts' that are in themselves silent.

A little girl was brought along for a consultation because she had suffered for years from intense pains in one of her legs, which ultimately prevented her from sleeping; sometimes she would scream out in agony. An organic cause had already been ruled out. The mother then told me that she often became irritated and swore at the girl. She said that she (the mother) had serious problems with her teeth; it was impossible to fit any appliance because she ground down all her prostheses until they 'broke'. The girl was also afraid of anything that burst or exploded, like balloons or fire-crackers; the mother added that sometimes she was so exasperated that she would have liked to kill her children. She said that her daughter often played a game in which a chick was left without a mummy because, when the hen was with the cock to start a family, along came a 'baddie' and killed the hen. She went on to describe her own sad experience as a girl with a mother who was always depressed and never devoted any time to her.

A link immediately formed in my mind. Unknown to herself, the mother was inhabited by a 'pit bull terrier' which constantly bit 'her daughter's leg', making her scream with pain. For me, this was like a scene from a film, which I could see before me although its phases were in the wrong order: the bleeding leg and the biting pit bull terrier. In other words, this was the story of a little girl who was wounded and in pain because her mother's mind was so occupied with the pit bull terrier that she had no room in it for her daughter, who, instead, was a burden she would rather have had dead. However, it was also the story of her own childhood: inside her was a 'transgenerational' pit bull terrier, inherited from the contact with her depressed mother (Faimberg 1988, Kaës et al. 1993).

Naturally, all this could not be expressed so directly, but it was a hypothesis that made sense of the situation and organized the field.

The analyst's α function had formed images; the 'apparatus for thinking thoughts' had woven a possible narration (the fruit of a reverie); and what had appeared meaningless began to assume a possible organizing structure. Once this dish had been prepared in the 'analytic kitchen', it had of course – if confirmed – to be served up in the 'analytic restaurant' in the appropriate form and at the appropriate time.

Let us now turn to an issue that has received increasing attention in recent years – namely, that of the analyst as a person. This problem has in fact been almost completely solved by the work of Willy and Madeleine Baranger, starting with their famous paper of 1961–62. The thesis is that, in field terms – even in older formulations that were surely much less sophisticated than today's – the presence and constellation of anxieties and defences in the analyst 'co-structures' the field together with the patient. Apart from the work of the Barangers (Baranger and Baranger 1961–62, 1964, 1969), the relevant literature includes two Argentine publications (Kancyper 1990, 1997) and my own earlier contributions on the subject (Ferro 1992, 1993c, 1994b, 1994c, 1994d, 1994e, 1994f, 1994g, 1996d, 1996e, 1999c, 2000a, 2000c, 2003).

The important aspect here is the part played by the analyst's mental functioning day by day – for the analyst's mode of functioning in the session, characterized by greater or lesser receptivity, greater or lesser reverie and greater or lesser narrative competence, partly determines the form assumed by the session itself. Again, whereas on the one hand the analyst's mental 'dysfunction' is a painful fact for the patient, on the other it is a precious and inexhaustible source of information on the mating of the two minds and on the patient's constant renarration of everything that occurs.

On one occasion when I was emotionally blocked with a woman patient, instead of adopting my usual attitude of receptive listening, I found myself interpreting like a river in full flood. The patient failed to turn up for her next session. She later told me that, because the Ticino was in flood, many roads were not negotiable, and she had felt it wiser to stay at home until the blockage caused by the inundation was over. She then told me of her intention to take a 't'ai chi' course. What better way could there be of telling the analyst to keep quiet (*taci* in Italian) than by skipping sessions and then playing a linguistic game with the similar sounds of 't'ai chi' (slow, relaxing gymnastics) and *taci* (pronounced almost identically in Italian)?

At about the same time, a male patient of mine dreamed of a man who was becoming increasingly lean and dry and a butcher attacking some cows with a big knife, causing them to scream out in pain. He associated to the dreams (or rather, he interpreted them for himself) by saying that in the last few days I had seemed to him drier and 'sharper' than usual and that this had caused him a lot of pain. In this way, by giving me a beating, he succeeded in putting me in touch with the origin of 'my blockage' and helped me, without any self-disclosure on my part, to regain the appropriate mental attitude.

However, does this mean that the analyst's mental attitude ought to be totally stable at all times? It certainly does not. Does it mean that we can or should allow ourselves to be 'treated' by our patients? Once again, definitely not.

It actually means that we must be aware that our mind is a variable of the field and that the patient, once again as our best colleague, can help us (usually unwittingly) by drawing our attention to a 'bursting of the banks' or 'ill-being' on our part, for which we are bound to assume responsibility. We must then work with ourselves to regain our usual attitude as quickly as possible.

My supervision work has increasingly convinced me that, the more that analysts are dominated by an ego ideal (Widlöcher 1978), or rather by a demanding analytic superego, the less they will be able to place themselves in the service of their patients, tolerating their defences and their receiving capacity and accepting the indications that patients give; instead the analysts will act as a 'crusader' of the presumed truth in their possession, 'anointed' as they are by some psychoanalytic theory or other – usually a highly orthodox one – which they espouse in a kind of orgiastic and complaisant primal scene. If not prepared to join in the game, the patient is seen as defensive, resistant, aggressive, envious and unsuitable for analysis.

It is not unusual for young, or even not so young, analysts to be filled with this sacred fury. Hard work is necessary to make them once again capable of listening to the patient's productions modestly, attentively and respectfully, 'without memory or desire', and in particular without fearing that the creativity sometimes required constitutes culpable heresy (Kernberg 1993).

I should like to mention here an exciting clinical case that came to my attention. It concerned the therapy of a boy with Asperger's syndrome, in which the flexibility, creativity and courage of an analyst who was anything but naïve made for growth and profound transformation; however, the analyst had needed for a long time to forgo many of his usual interpretive strategies in order to find the right way of 'reaching' this patient authentically and thus enabling him to develop.

It is no coincidence that it is often child analysts who are most capable of 'creative transgressions', because little patients (and indeed seriously ill patients) are refractory to any form of 'education' (Ferruta et al. 2000; Norman 2001; Vallino Macciò, 1998). For this reason, I would recommend every analyst to have the experience of at least one child analysis. In this connection, it is surely significant that in the last few years nearly all psychoanalytic societies have succeeded in organizing comprehensive training courses in child and adolescent analysis.

2

THE CULTURE OF REVERIE AND THE CULTURE OF EVACUATION

Lorenzo

Lorenzo was a boy who, although all of 8 years old, would eat only liquid or puréed foods. He would not accept anything solid. At school he was extremely inhibited and had no friends. He also had the odd characteristic of constantly asking his mother 'Why?' about everything. Lorenzo's mother had had two bereavements in quick succession: when Lorenzo was 2 years old, her father had died, and before that she had lost her husband when the boy was 1 year old. Since then she had been intensely depressed, but had had to continue with her office job to make ends meet.

In the first session Lorenzo drew a picture which he said depicted an isolated, gloomy, dark and desolate house – 'perhaps with no doors,' he added. He then remained sitting motionless, thoroughly blocked like a car with the handbrake on. However, on seeing the toy box, he seemed to liven up. After asking if he really could use the figures inside it, he suddenly embarked on a game in which they set about each other violently; the most terrible of all was the one he called the 'ripper dog'.

When I commented that this dog must be terribly hungry, he picked up two of the figures and had them mime a mixture of fighting and copulation, saying that the woman 'mustn't take off her bra'. He then drew the picture reproduced in Figure 2.1, showing a dinosaur, a prehistoric bird, a rocket and, at the bottom, a little man in a boat.

All of a sudden, Lorenzo's drama became clear to me: a depressed mother was like a gloomy, dark house which perhaps lacked any door or other means of entry. Of course, the characters beating each other up could be seen from various viewpoints, but my choice would be the representation of the clash between the child's proto-emotional needs (in other words, his projective identifications) and a closed mind that was available only ostensibly because of the intensity of the depression; the doors were in effect just 'pretend' doors drawn in with a pencil.

13

Figure 2.1

This illustrates the general principle that, if 'projective identifications' do not find a receiving and transforming space but instead encounter a negative reverie (Ferro 1987, 1991b, 1992, 1998c, 2000b, 2003, Ferro and Meregnani 1994, 1998; Ribeiro de Moraes 1999), they turn back on the subject, magnified to gigantic proportions, and remain in the state of dinosaur or rocket emotions. All that is necessary is for there to be a mind that understands and accepts, at however minimal a level, that the hunger for a relationship is mimed by the combination of fighting and copulation – a relationship that must be 'protected' because the other might otherwise be ripped apart.

The drawing also depicts the beginnings of a containing and transforming function, in the form of the little man steering the boat (see Figure 2.2).

Having found an open mind, Lorenzo for the first time had an opportunity of narrating his own traumatic history, and he was able to find a place for the 'ripper dog' against which anorexia and inhibition were inevitable defences, there being no other possible way of managing this monster. The constant questioning – 'Why?' – was of course an attempt to open up the mother's mind and make it accessible. The story continued by way of battles between Indian tribes butchering each other and atrocities of all kinds, until the eventual arrival of an 'ambassador' who began to lay down rules for the game, which gradually turned into a violent rugby championship.

14

Figure 2.2

Here now are some reflections.

The human mind needs to relate to the other in order to develop (Ogden 1997, 2001). Bion gives an admirable description of this initial switching on of the human mind, which is tantamount to a 'big bang' of thought in the encounter between the projection of primitive anxieties (β elements) and a mind that is capable of receiving and transforming them (reverie) and that 'transmits' not only the 'finished product' (the decontaminated anxieties, or β elements transformed into α elements), but also, and in my view most im-portantly of all, *the method of making such transformations* (the α function) (Bion 1962, 1963, 1965). According to this view, even the unconscious is an entity consequent upon the relationship with the available other.

A little girl in analysis once made me a drawing which – apart from its relational meaning at the time – I see as an extraordinary portrayal of my own present model of the formation of the unconscious (Figure 2.3).

It shows a sky represented by a mass of twisted, tangled threads, forming multicoloured skeins, and a sea of coloured lines seemingly woven in an orderly manner into a kind of weft. The whole picture conveys a powerful impression of motion, which stems from a boat positioned in the centre that contains three people. In shuttling from one side of the paper to the other, the boat seems to interweave the turbulence of the top with the threads at the bottom. The more the boat shuttles back and forth, the more the lower part of the picture seems to expand, but, at the same time, the more the top has to be woven. In other words, what matters is apparently the weaving capacity of the boat's occupants. There is no ultimate landing place, except the expansion of the weavable, of the woven fabric and of

Figure 2.3

the capacity to weave – or, leaving the metaphor behind, an expansion of the thinkable, of thought and of the capacity to think. This tellingly exemplifies Bion's well-known thesis that psychoanalysis is like a probe that expands the field it is investigating, so that, the further we penetrate into the unconscious, the more work awaits us. This drawing in my view illustrates how the introjected α function (the fruit of relationship) permits constant transformation of proto-emotional turbulence into thought and thinkable emotions.

I am concerned here mainly with the qualities the other's mind must have: the capacity to receive, to leave in abeyance, to metabolize, to return the elaborated product to the subject and, in particular, to 'transmit the method'. This is achieved by returning the product in unsaturated form and allowing the subject's mind as it were to learn its trade in the workshop of the other's.

The first operation, which is totally creative, original and artistic, is the formation of a visual pictogram (the α element), while the second is to make a narration out of the sequence of α elements. Subsequent functions will be introjection of the tolerability of frustration, of the capacity to mourn, of time and of limits. All this takes place by way of the 'mental' quality activated in the relationship with the mother and father – for I believe that reverie may be equally maternal or paternal (Ferro 1992). The 'cultural' problem today in my opinion concerns the importance, space and time to be assigned to these operations, which have to do with the development of the mind out of the 'available mental quality of the other' (Guignard 1996).

Unlike other species with their largely programmed instinctive behaviours, humankind has a drama – the drama of possessing a mind that develops over a long raising period. What might be described as failure of the process of mental development results in a range of pathologies extending from hallucinations and psychosomatic illness to characteropathic and criminal behaviour – all of which are ways of evacuating and discharging primitive anxieties that have not been worked through.

It seems to me, then, that it is not the 'mind' that governs the instincts, with human reason ruling over the world of the drives, but that the specific problem for humans is precisely the opposite – namely, that they have a mind with all its peculiarities. What gives rise to violent and antisocial behaviour is the existence of a mind that has been unable to develop. The violence originates not from instinct but from a suffering mind that disturbs the harmonious functioning of the human beast's behaviour: if people did not have a mind, they would be a functioning primate. The problem of humankind is the mind and its rudimentary nature – and, in particular, the fact that, in order to develop properly, that mind needs years of care. A dysfunctional mind leads to violence and destruction as the only way of evacuating β elements (Ferro 1993a, 1993b, 1996b, 1997, 2001a, 2001c).

A functioning mind is one that continuously creates images (α elements) out of proto-emotions and proto-sensations, and that metabolizes everything it receives into factors of creativity; it creates dream thought and, from it, dreams and thought. When a mind does not operate in this receiving/transforming/creative mode, its mode of functioning is reversed.

Culture in my view impacts on the mind at various points. There is a *relational microculture* which is also micro-environmental, which constitutes the part of the boat in Figure 2.3 that represents the mind's α function and oedipal function, on which the development of the capacity for thought of every human child within his or her environment depends. However, there is also a *social macroculture* (within which the relational microcultures live in a kind of osmosis), towards which we cannot claim to be indifferent. A central issue is the extent to which the social macroculture acknowledges the mental and emotional, the vital importance of relationship to the development of the mind, as well as the space and time that culture allows for making available the functions of reverie, fantasy and dreaming.

There is always the risk of a purging of affects, often for the sake of supposed scientific objectivity. Whereas this trend is evident on a large scale in the social field, I also see it as a serious threat to psychoanalysis, which ought instead to be turning to account the 'specificity' of the human animal.

In Chapter XVI of *Learning from Experience*, Bion had already noted that scientific techniques gave their best results when applied to inanimate objects;

of course, the three basic links between x that wished to know and y that wished to be known – x L y, x H y and x K y – 'cease to exist in proportion as inanimate machinery is introduced to displace the living element' (Bion 1962, p. 48).

However, Bion (1965) also points out that the emotions permeating the other's mind are fundamental determinants of mental development and constitute the connective tissue in which mental contents are set, so that they also determine whether they tend towards K or –K, or towards ♀ ♂ or –(♀ ♂).

Tranquillo Cremona's painting *Mother Love* (Figure 2.4) is in my view a good pictographic example of the culture of reverie.

Figure 2.4 L'Amore Materno reproduced with permission of Civiche Raccolte d'Arte, Milano.

A partially functioning capacity for reverie seems to me to be well represented by one of William Blake's illustrations for Dante's *Divine Comedy*, which shows a mother receiving a little girl, while more primitive aspects are rejected and eliminated by projection (giving rise to Jekyll and Hyde type splits) (Figure 2.5).

I suggest that a totally inadequate capacity for reverie is portrayed by another Blake painting (*The Great Red Dragon and the Woman Clothed in the Sun*), which conjures up monstrous aspects of the mind that do not meet with a sufficient capacity for reverie but only with a fragile and inadequate maternal function (Figure 2.6).

The harm done by insufficient reverie can be illustrated in narrative form by the literary and social phenomenon of Thomas Harris's (1981, 1988, 1999) trilogy on the violent history of a serial killer, in which uncontainable suffering is evacuated by acting out.

The first book, *Red Dragon*, tells the story of the tragic childhood of Francis Dolarhyde, abandoned by his mother and with a face so badly disfigured that he dare not look in a mirror. An attempt to return to his mother and her new family fails wretchedly, and his career of carnage begins after his grandmother's death. It goes on until he meets a 'blind' girl, who is not alienated by his facial deformity, and with whom he has an affectionate relationship in which he is fully accepted. The result is, in effect, a split between one aspect irrevocably bent on revenge – the 'Red Dragon' – and another, his 'true' self, that wishes to save the girl and the tender relationship that has arisen between them.

The second book, *The Silence of the Lambs*, is also about a serial killer, Jame Gumb, who kills big women; he too has a background of abandonment and trauma. He kills because he wants to make himself a suit of female human skin, to serve as a 'new skin and identity'. He murders these young women so as to construct this integument for himself, just like a tailor.

A character present in both novels is Dr Lecter, a psychiatrist-and-serial-killer incarcerated in a cage in a maximum-security prison. Officer Starling, the heroine of the second novel, sets about hunting for the killer with the aid of Dr Lecter, who forms an almost protective relationship with her. This emerges clearly in the third novel, *Hannibal* (Hannibal is also the first name of Dr Lecter, who becomes that book's hero). *Hannibal* describes Officer Starling's attempts to 'arrest' Lecter after his escape from prison. However, over and above the genre of the horror story cum detective novel, what is narrated is the story of the vicissitudes of Dr Lecter's childhood. We are told that he lost a beloved little sister at a tender age. Falling victim to cannibalistic acts, she was eaten by a gang of starving bandits who broke into the family farm and, finding nothing else on which to feed, devoured not only a scraggy deer but also the little girl, in the absence of parents who might have been able to defend the children.

This trauma, it seems, has to be repeated 'actively': as an adult, Dr Lecter in turn becomes a cannibal. He would like to reverse the flow of time and bring

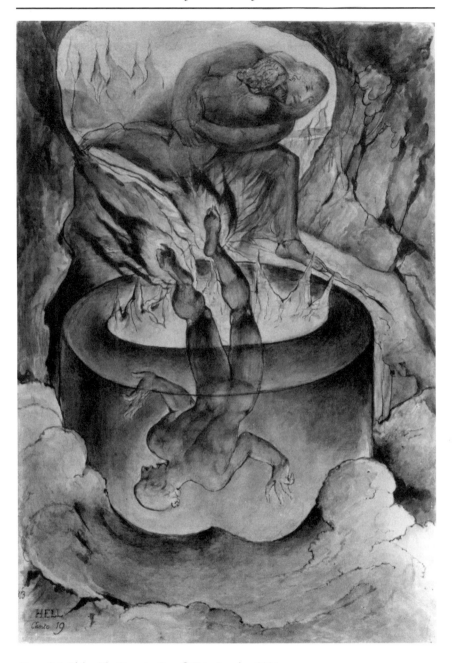

Figure 2.5 Blake, *The Simoniac Pope* © Tate, London 2004

Figure 2.6 Blake, *The Red Dragon and the Woman Clothed with the Sun*, Brooklyn Musuem of Art, gift of William Augustus White

his little sister back to life, making time non-linear. Officer Starling could perhaps serve partly as a substitute and partly as a 'depository' for the sister, if only time could run backwards and the sister come alive again. The cannibalistic scene is repeated until the novel reaches a terrifying climax: a man Lecter sees as guilty – he himself, for not having been able to save his little sister – undergoes a brain operation and, while wide awake, partakes of a meal of his own brain, which is sliced through in the frontal lobes, cooked and eaten – just as he himself gnaws at his brain out of guilt.

This perhaps illustrates what happens in the absence of 'food for the mind' – that is, of reverie. The tender, affectionate parts (the little sister, the capacity for ♀) are destroyed by violent parts that ultimately cannibalize the mind itself; others are then made to atone as victims. Had there been food – reverie – the sister could have stayed alive, the affects and emotions could have found a place, and Dr Lecter would not have been a victim and executioner devoured by guilt and at the same time an avenging angel. The criminals of the beginning of the story can be seen as β elements which, in the absence of reverie and transformation (by an α function), cannibalize the mind.

The first book's serial killer can thus be regarded as portraying the need to evacuate trauma-related emotions by violent acting out, the violence seeking a container which, however, proves inadequate: the persecutory bad objects force him to exact revenge, until he finds the loving girl, so that there is a split between the psychotic part and the 'part capable of relationship'. The unreceived and untransformed aspects give rise to madness and persecution, just as the second book describes an attempt to find a psychic skin, a container capable of 'taking inside' (a ♀ able to accommodate ♂). Finally, the most alarming character of all emerges: in effect the 'director' of all these stories, namely the mad psychiatrist, the embodiment of the archaic superego, who devours everything on account of his intolerable sense of guilt, which ultimately impels him to desperate, harmful – and indeed self-harmful – action. This sequence of three books is in my view a modern myth that perfectly illustrates the absence of primary care and its consequences – namely, the killer, the attempt at self-therapy (the skin) and persecutory guilt.

We are of course not sociologists. The main focus of our attention is on the mini-killer phenomena represented by the reversal of the normal flow of projective identification (from child to adult, or from patient to analyst) and by negative reveries, which, precisely, kill off any possibility of development of the mind and of the species and which may also be attributable to suffering parents through no fault of their own, or to analysts who in turn are not culpable but simply 'fanatical'.

3

CONTAINER INADEQUACY AND VIOLENT EMOTIONS

Andrea

At our first meeting, Andrea filled sheet after sheet of paper with drawings of dinosaurs, which he then crossed out completely and replaced by little tortoises (Figure 3.1).

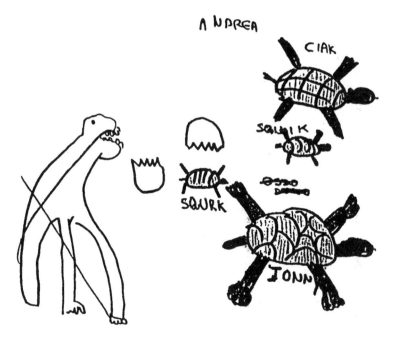

Figure 3.1

Andrea was brought to me for a consultation owing to his sudden outbursts of anger and frequent threats to harm or perhaps even kill himself. He was described by his parents as a boy who never played, had no friends, and was solitary and sad. There was something effeminate about his appearance.

The mother seemed rigid and controlled, while the father was absent from the family's emotional life. Both disappeared after the first consultation, but turned up again after several months.

At this second meeting, the mother said that fortunately, in the new school year, Andrea's class consisted 'almost entirely of girls, as lots of boys had left'. However, she added that since Christmas Andrea had been afraid of being alone, even for a very short time, and that he suffered from insomnia – or rather, he would fall asleep quickly and then wake up in the middle of the night with terrifying nightmares, causing him to seek refuge in his parents' bedroom. The mother went on to say that Andrea was afraid of 'story time' at school (when he had to make up stories in class) and had problems with writing, and in particular with spelling, which he kept on changing.

Andrea arrived at our next meeting with a cry of 'Wow! It's all different! That's nice!' He was referring to some changes in the consulting room's furniture since our first meeting some months before. This time, Andrea began by making a drawing (Figure 3.2) of himself in a room afraid to go to sleep (where are the dinosaurs?); a second drawing followed an appreciative comment by the analyst (Figure 3.3).

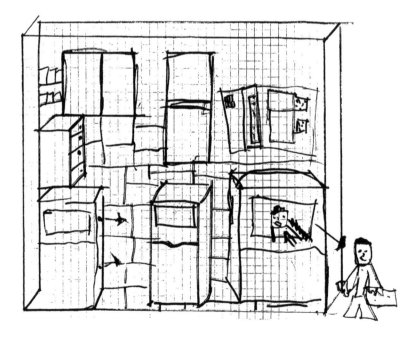

Figure 3.2

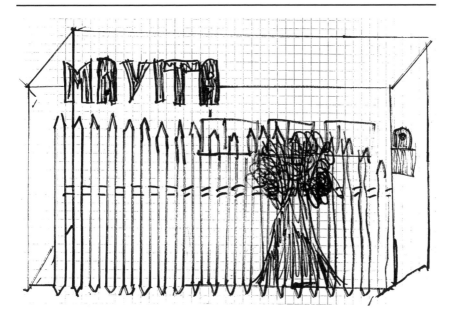

Figure 3.3

The end of the session was somewhat unusual: Andrea's mother was more than ten minutes late calling for him and, all of a sudden, cries were heard from the staircase; after a while Andrea said he thought he recognized his mother's voice. Hurrying out of the room, I found that Andrea's mother was stuck in the lift, crying out . . . to be released!

I shall now attempt to show how the possible variants of the plot conceal a kind of *fabula* with a significant structure. The *plot* is the story as told, while the *fabula* is the underlying sequence of narrated situations.

Andrea had narrated his drama immediately: inside him were emotions that were so primitive and violent (the dinosaurs) that the only way he could deal with them was to shut them, or perhaps *himself*, up in a rigid container – what Meltzer (1992) would call a claustrum (the tortoises). However, these contents, being so compressed inside the claustrum ($\male \female ; \male \xrightarrow{\text{compressed}} \female$), periodically caused the claustrum itself to explode (the outbursts of anger and despair) (see note on p. 35). The pressurized, unshareable emotions were segregated; they needed to be surrounded by armour, or else they were split off and expelled, while Andrea took refuge in the claustrum.

Even if the mother was unable to supply reverie and $\female$ to her son, she was well able to choose significant and indeed illuminating facts in her narration. I see her comment 'Lots of boys had left' as describing the lightening of the pressurized contents or proto-emotions ♂ that had been split off, allowing the containers (girls) to withstand the – now lighter – pressure. However, these fragments of 'contained' (♂♂♂ – i.e. these proto-emotions), although split off, remained in orbit and returned as terrifying presences when Andrea was alone or it was time for him to go to sleep. The parents' presence was needed as an antidote to this return of the ♂'s, which were terrifying because they did not meet with an adequate container function (♀).

'Story time' (without the 'barriers' of rules) was feared because it might allow these split-off fragments to 'return', and when they did they sought refuge in Andrea's spelling, which was disrupted by them as if by an earthquake.

Andrea rejoiced on noticing a change that seemed to exemplify the capacity of the analyst's mind to effect transformations. The second drawing was apparently made up of sarcophagi which could afford protection and shelter; these were the shells of the tortoises. He had to stay hidden in his sarcophagus because the split-off dinosaurs (unthinkable proto-emotional contents) might burst in at any time. The analyst's presence and the non-persecutory climate of the session transformed Andrea's mental climate: the armoured claustrum turned into an open fence, and something now flowered – a non-worrying, non-dinosaur emotion that was nevertheless alive – as was the warm relationship embodied in the letters VIT, which seemed to be saying '*Tu sei la VITA MIA*' ('You are MY LIFE'); that is, something that made him feel good and allowed him to think in terms of, and to hope for, changes (Figure 3.3). The final scene with the mother in the lift was like a product of fantasy, repeating as it did the central theme of an emotional explosion inside a claustrum from which the subject wished to be rescued so as to find a container.

However, let us return to the clinical sequence. Some drawings from subsequent sessions are reproduced here.

In one session, on hearing a noise, Andrea was anxious that it might be coming from the *Tyrannosaurus rex* he was drawing (Figure 3.4), which had what looked like tree roots instead of legs.

The analyst was quick to interpret that maybe Rex had found somewhere to put down roots and had calmed down.

Next came a drawing of a little dinosaur, on which Andrea superimposed human eyes and a human nose and mouth (Figure 3.5), indicating that a further transformation was under way.

Not everything always went smoothly in Andrea's analysis. There were periods of turbulence, long stretches when the analyst felt sleepy, and situations of stasis or repetition, but gradually it became possible to metabolize the 'dinosaurs'. After a year of treatment, Andrea's mother told me that his outbursts of anger had ceased and that he was no longer violent. At the end of the therapy she also claimed to be unable to remember why Andrea had come into analysis in the first place: 'He was surely never a violent child.'

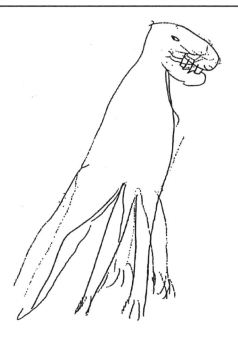

Figure 3.4

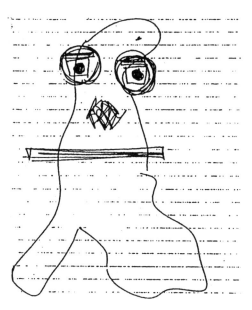

Figure 3.5

The important point here is surely that the container ♀ is stressed by a particularly turbulent 'contained', thus giving rise to 'cracks' in the container itself ♀̣, which have to do with the 'terror' of explosion (e.g. that resulting from the panic attack?). In consequence, the 'fragmented container' is transformed into ♂ ('the projected contained'), which intrudes violently.

This can be illustrated clinically by the example of a patient who said he felt like 'a murderous rabbit that kills everyone when it is terrified' (see Figure 3.6, which shows the transformation of a fragmented container into an invasive 'contained').

Finally, let us consider a clinical situation that involved a failure of the analyst's capacity for reverie and a reversal of the flow of projective identifications (Ferro and Meregnani 1998).

One day at 5.30 p.m. I finished a session with a psychotic little girl that left me with a powerful residue of anxiety. Doing my best to recover my usual mental attitude, I began the next session at 6 p.m. with a sensitive, sufficiently 'healthy' adult woman patient. My mind seemed to be cluttered and I had a sensation of awkwardness and ill-being. Gradually freeing myself from this, I felt better and the session took its course.

The next morning the patient recounted a blood-curdling dream, which had greatly surprised her because it came at a time of well-being and satisfaction. As a little girl, she was walking up a hill in her local park with some friends. They went to the bar to buy ice cream, but decided to have orange juice instead. Then came the horrifying part: with an air of total normality, the barman picked up some little girls' heads instead of oranges, squeezed them and expected the youngsters to drink the resulting stringy, whitish juice. They fled in terror.

The constant dialectic between the development of ♀ and ♂, between a favourable environment and the capacity to develop new thoughts, is also reflected, although its author is no doubt completely unaware of it, in a 'black' novel (which immediately found a place in Gallimard's famous *série noire*) – namely, Giuseppe Ferrandino's *Pericle il nero* (1993). This is the extraordinary

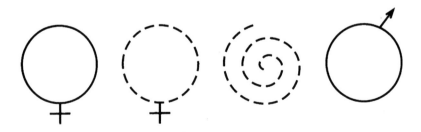

Figure 3.6

story of the birth of a thought, and with it of the capacity to think, in someone suffering from a severe characteropathic perversion.

The hero, Pericle, is incapable of metaphor even on the linguistic level; his attitude to people is 'up yours' – and he puts this into practice literally, sodomizing to order people in whom he is required to induce feelings of shame and humiliation as a warning. He acts out of instinct, saves himself instinctively from an attempt on his life, and responds to every stimulus with an equal and opposite reaction. Thus Newton's third law of motion (to every action there is an equal and opposite reaction) seems to apply also to the characteropathic mind. Having often got into trouble with his criminal gang, he manages to get away and save himself without ever having a plan or a thought, but simply goes where circumstances take him, guided by a certain primordial flair for avoiding danger.

One day, however, a meeting with a Polish woman in effect gives rise to a human story that sows the seeds for the birth of a thought. It is her affectionate gesture in ruffling his hair that creates a space in his head for an imaginative scene. For the first time, at her house, he reacts to a frustration by *imagining* the committing of an atrocity: although what he imagines is indeed an atrocity, he does not *actually* commit it.

The author gives a remarkable description of how his hero, unable to control frustrations, operates in reflex-arc mode (stimulus and response) until the modifying neuron between stimulus and response appears in the form of the proto-apparatus for thinking thoughts and hence for imagining. Pericle finds it so impossible to tolerate frustration, and is so sensitive to the climate of the moment, that the slightest indication of the non-availability of the 'Polish woman' causes him to leave her and return to the scenario of his original vicissitudes. Acting with characteropathic violence, he gets the better of those who wish him dead, and has obtained an appreciable sum of money by illicit means. He is about to subject another defeated enemy to his sodomitic ritual using his customary antibiotic cream (thinking it will protect him from possible contagion), when he suddenly sees the entire scene from a different perspective and decides not to proceed.

Here again a thought is born, bearing witness to the development of the capacity to think that thought, and we glimpse the possibility of a different future with the Polish woman, on whose doorstep he proposes to turn up with enough money for them to start a new life together in Poland. Perhaps the project will bear fruit. Meanwhile he succeeds in breaking with the basic-assumption mode of mental functioning and in understanding that the only way to emerge from a dead-end situation is the transgression of thought (Gaburri 1982; Gaburri and Ferro 1988), whereby he can breathe life into something of his own, different from the group culture by which he had always been pervaded and which had 'acted him out'. In other words, the birth of a thought coincides with the transgressive birth of an 'individual identity'. As the story unfolds, it is remarkable to see how the author also portrays the changes in

Pericle's use of language as reflecting his progressive access to metaphor and symbolism, as he relinquishes the prison of concrete language and acting out.

The change of scenery . . .

Some of the most precious moments in analytic work are observed when a change of scenery takes place – as if one were watching a film about Ancient Rome and all of a sudden Red Cloud or General Custer appeared. This is the irruption of a new, previously unthinkable 'selected fact' (Bion 1963), which can now reorganize the entire scene into a different *Gestalt* bearing witness to the non-linear development that betokens profound transformation.

Nicoletta

Nicoletta began her analysis as the victim of abuse, bullying and injustice. However, there came a session in which she told me how she had 'ground her teeth down in fury at keeping quiet'. She described how she had had four collisions within a few days due to not having 'braked in time', and then mentioned a fellow she met outside the consulting-room door, perhaps a patient who was in analysis to help him control himself, and who could not tolerate being shut in. Next she spoke about her brother, who had told her that she would be capable of killing, and said that, a few years before, she had started to dress differently, changing from a 'short skirt and stiletto heels' to a 'nun's style' out of a sense of guilt.

All this suggested possible reasons for her wanting to have analysis: to meet and learn how to control the 'killer' – her own violent, uncontrolled functioning – who was finally able to enter the sessions, however marginally, in the form of the accidents ('not braking in time') and was then personified by the 'man waiting outside' – a claustrophobe who was like a Doberman with a muzzle-as-claustrum. All the many sessions that had preceded this one had served only for the 'development of the container', as illustrated in Figure 3.7.

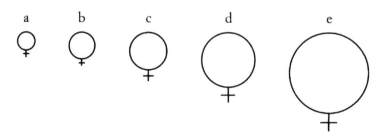

Figure 3.7

Only the formation of container (e) allows 'Ki', or rather $\overset{\male}{\circledcirc}$, the 'killer-contained', to find an environment in which to assume emotional reality. In other words, $\male$ can attain thinkability only if there has been appropriate development of $\female$. This gives rise to a complete change of scenery, as if, in a film about a nunnery, Genghis Khan were suddenly to arrive and be allowed in! In the present case, Nicoletta was able for the first time to have non-persecutory access to her wish to kill her father, of which she had several times become aware.

Again, the contained is $\overset{\male}{\circledcirc}$ – that is, a 'killer-contained' that cannot be represented in thought as long as $\female$ is inadequate; i.e. as long as the contained is more violent and explosive than the capacity for thinking it.

. . . that is, when the container explodes

Carlo

My patient Carlo was very afraid of 'losing control' and used a defensive strategy based on rationalization. At the end of one session, a comment 'slipped out' to the effect that it might be possible to say everything one thought, including negative things and even criticisms of one's analyst.

In the next session he brought a dream of a southern-looking man of whom he was afraid, a woman who seemed to be making advances to him and a girl in the family way with little brats around her. This dream could have been interpreted on various levels, with the emphasis ranging from the oedipal aspect to the feared split-off parts, but could also usefully be construed as a precise description of what was happening in the analytic consulting room. In these terms, he was beginning to experience the wish – almost the seductive temptation – to let himself go and tell his story; although this idea attracted him, he was afraid of the 'southern-looking man' who represented the more passionate level.

There was a $\female$ that was beginning to be thought of as attractive, but also the fear of even more terrifying 'containeds', which might not be containable ($\male$), even given the idea of an expanding container $\female\female\female\female$ (the pregnant girl) and the expectation of little brats (thoughts in search of a thinker, or β or balpha elements waiting to be alphabetized). This is illustrated in Figure 3.8.

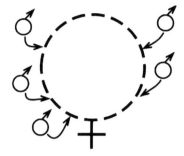

Figure 3.8

Overstressing the container

The early approach of a split

A female analysand mentioned a 13-year-old boy who had come to her for help at the surgery where she worked as a general practitioner. He was, she said, good at school, but suffered from asthma attacks and found it difficult to get on with his friends. The analyst interpreted that she had made the acquaintance of an adolescent part of herself which, while well adapted, was expressing the need for more freedom.

In the next session, the patient said that she had had a disturbance of vision: for several minutes on end, she had lost the sense of three-dimensionality and had seen a bothersome halo around everything she saw; she had feared that she might be suffering from a hemianopsia and might no longer be able to read lines of text on a page, but had then felt better after relaxing and eating a little sugar. She went on to talk about a crazy friend with yellow hair who kept rambling on, and a little girl who wept in desperation on failing to recognize her mother after she had had a haircut.

What had happened?

The analyst had been confronted with the problem of a split in time (the teenage boy), which he had approached by bringing it down to the same level: 'Tell me about the adolescent aspects of yourself.'

Tackling splits not only in time but also in space (for example, when a patient says: 'My cousin . . .') is indeed one of the analyst's tasks. However, it is important for this to be done gradually, as if one were treating a V-shaped wound and needed to stitch the edges together gradually, but starting from the apex. My over-hasty stitching had triggered the situation described by the patient in the next session: she had lost her sense of the three-dimensionality of time, had seen her own image flattened, and suffered from a 'halo' effect that had interfered with her clarity of vision; as a result, she had lost the possibility of understanding and following the text of what the analyst had said.

She had then relaxed and cheered up. The crisis of disorientation was over, but continued with the story of an unrecognizable friend, as alien as the analyst had become after the interpretation. The subsequent transformation (the little girl who could not recognize her mother because her appearance had changed) was a token of the patient's suffering due to something that had made her lose contact with the known analyst and put her in touch with an unfamiliar element that had generated excessive anxiety.

It is therefore worth devoting some thought not only to the appropriate way of tackling splits (whether in space or in time) but also to the patient's constant renarration of the analyst's interpretations, so that the analyst can constantly modulate his intepretive activity (Barale and Ferro 1992; Bezoari and Ferro 1991a, 1991b, 1994b; Ferro 1991a, 1996c, 1999c, 1999d, 2001c). This last function can, in my view, only seldom be usefully interpreted, but becomes a guiding line that helps the person at the helm to stay on course.

So far I have considered what happens when the container is inadequate or overstressed, as well as how new and often unpredictable narrations can follow on from its development. I should now like to turn to the opposite situation, in which the container is ready but there is an initial deficiency in the contained, due to interpretive inadequacy on the part of the analyst.

In praise of the contained

A young woman patient was talking about her new, disappointing boyfriend, who was aloof and had several times proved impotent. The analyst did not interpret these communications within the relationship and confined himself to some very cautious comments.

I told the young supervisee concerned that he should take the stage in a different way, as a 'hussar', adopting a more active, incisive stance and touching the patient with more active interpretations, if possible of the transference. The candidate reported that in the next session he had still remained on the margin of the scene. The patient had therefore raised the stakes by presenting her boyfriend as increasingly scatter-brained and suffering from erection problems. I again stressed to my young colleague that he should act like a hussar, and helped him to work through his difficulty in so doing. In the next session he was active, producing a large number of focused interpretations, many of them of the transference.

In his description of the session, he mentioned an image produced by the patient: she had fantasized seeing a large number of concentric circles. Good heavens, I thought, he has over-interpreted: the patient had talked about a 'target', saying she had felt excessively 'in his sights' – but then, to my great relief, I heard that the patient had continued her account in a way that could not have been predicted: 'These concentric circles remind me of focusing a pair of binoculars we once had: my mother could watch me walking along a difficult path and I was pleased, as I had a sense of well-being and felt that I was not alone.' She had gone on to describe her boyfriend's sexual reawakening, which had exceeded all expectations.

33

Cracks and fractures in the field

Microfractures in communication, like caesuras and withdrawals, are of fundamental importance because they give rise to cracks or pivots whereby what was
previously outside the present relationship in the form of a set of 'undigested
facts' can burst into it – in other words, because they allow the transference to
become the engine of the analysis, by contributing raw material from the
patient's internal world and history. If this 'disembarkation' is to be useful and
constructive, it must take a gradual form; to some extent at least, 'bridgeheads'
must have been established and the present situation of the relationship must
'hold', absorb and transform these vital but often explosive charges.

If there are no cracks, the analysis will become sterile, bogged down in
an impasse, but if there are too many, all the various forms of negative and
psychotic transference will arise. From this point of view, the analyst is like a
dam controller who must modulate what 'enters' the metabolic cycle. Of
course, repressed, split-off, repudiated and undigested elements can make their
appearance through other channels too; their main vehicle is the projective
identifications that convey what has been experienced but not worked through
or thought and that bring it into the field.

The analyst's mind must also have this semi-permeable quality, so that it can
receive without being – excessively – invaded.

The model of the mind underlying this book is, I believe, clear. It combines the
'field' notions of Baranger and Baranger (1961–62), Bezoari and Ferro (1990a,
1990b, 1992, 1994a, 1999), Corrao (1992), Ferro (1992, 1996e, 1999a, 1999b)
and Gaburri (1997), with an expansion of some of Bion's concepts (Bion 1962,
1963, 1965). In this model, one part of the mind dreams while in the waking
state. Elements of this dream can be known through its narrative derivatives.
The 'contact barrier' is of fundamental importance in protecting us from
inundation by α, balpha and β elements (see Figures 3.9 and 3.10).

Both ♀♂ and Ps↔D act on the narrative derivative. More simply, any
turbulence in the field – even one due to an interpretation by the analyst –
generates (provided that the field holds firm and remains functional) α elements
that are inaccessible as such, but whose 'narrative derivatives' can be known; the
narrative derivative is a copy, albeit faint, of the α element (or sequence of α
elements).

Although the α element is in effect situated in an inaccessible room, there is
someone who can 'recount' it to me, or 'draw' or 'play' it or 'act it out' for me.
Attention to these narrative derivatives can greatly facilitate modulation of the
field and knowledge of its movements.

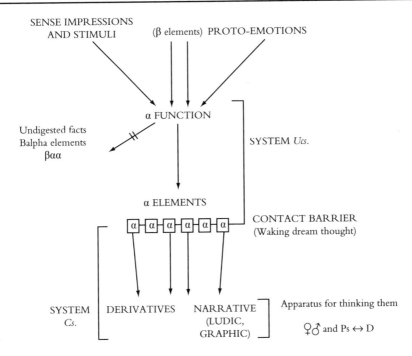

SENSE IMPRESSIONS
AND STIMULI

(β elements) PROTO-EMOTIONS

α FUNCTION

Undigested facts
Balpha elements
βαα

SYSTEM *Ucs.*

α ELEMENTS

CONTACT BARRIER
(Waking dream thought)

SYSTEM
Cs.

DERIVATIVES

NARRATIVE
(LUDIC,
GRAPHIC)

Apparatus for thinking them

♀♂ and Ps ↔ D

Figure 3.9

Note

In this chapter I use some personal symbols whose meaning will, I believe, be immediately evident:

♂ means a 'hyper-contained' that exceeds the capacity of a container.

☮ is a visual indication of the 'fragmentation' of the container and its transformation into a projected contained ♂ when it passes through ☮ (turbulence causing the container to fragment).

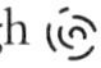

♀♀♀♀ represents the development of the container.

♂ represents a 'killer-contained' that destroys the holding capacity of the container.

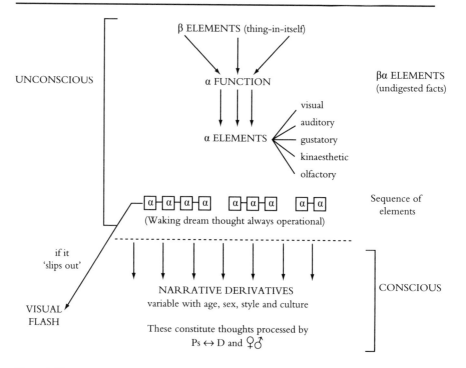

Figure 3.10

4

NACHTRÄGLICHKEIT AND THE STORK: THE ANALYTIC FIELD AND DREAM THOUGHT

The main themes on which my work has focused over the last few years all appear to a greater or lesser extent in this chapter: the various ways in which the 'characters' of the psychoanalytic session can be conceptualized; how the patient in effect constantly draws the analyst's attention to the functioning of the session itself; the continuous oscillation between interpretive activity and narrative transformations by the analyst; the development of Bion's concept of 'waking dream thought' and the eventual formulation of the concept of the 'narrative derivative' of this thought; and the importance of the micro-transformations in the here and now of the session on account of their capacity for ongoing modification of the patient's internal world by a continual series of instances of *Nachträglichkeit*, as well as for rewriting his history, sometimes in versions that 'never happened'.★

Again, I use clinical material not to 'demonstrate' anything but as a means of conveying and sharing the underlying theory – that is to say, in Bion's terms, as a means of talking about theory, but of doing so along Row C of the Grid, which is that of story-telling, dreams and private myths.

The authors by whom the development of my thought has been most strongly inspired are Baranger and Baranger and Bion (Bezoari and Ferro 1991b; Ferro 1992). They share one particular characteristic – namely, the

---

★ Translator's note: *Nachträglichkeit* is the term originally used by Freud for the process of retro-spective assignment of meaning rendered by Strachey in the *Standard Edition* as 'deferred action', a translation now generally agreed to be unsatisfactory. The French term *après-coup* is occasionally seen in an English-language context, but, in the absence of a generally accepted English equivalent, Freud's own word has been preferred here.

importance they attach to the functioning or dysfunctioning of the analyst's mental life in the session. Moreover, they do so differently from the American intersubjectivist school, which in my view lacks a clear-cut vision of the value to be assigned to unconscious mental functioning.

Baranger and Baranger (1961–62, 1969), authors of French origin who moved to South America, postulate that analyst and patient – or rather, their mental lives in the session – form a 'field', within which it is not at first possible to distinguish what belongs to one and what to the other. In fact, it is the area of unconscious collusion arising (the 'bulwark') that becomes the subject of the analyst's exploration and interpretation. Analysts must be capable of dissolving the 'mutual element of resistance' (the bulwark) by way of their 'second look', which enables them to distinguish themselves from the field to whose generation they have themselves contributed. In this way, interpretation constantly dissolves and reveals these constantly forming areas of collusion. Hence the task of analysts is the ongoing disentanglement of, and disentanglement of themselves from, the field that they unconsciously generate together with their patients.

Baranger and Baranger make projective identification a cornerstone of their proposed bipersonal metapsychology, developing the original Kleinian formulations in a direction remarkably consonant in many respects with the contributions of Bion. If projective identification is not merely an individual's omnipotent fantasy but something that really happens between two persons (Bion 1980), 'it is hardly surprising that it is of decisive importance for the structuring of any couple' (Baranger and Baranger 1961–62). The espousal of this radically bipersonal model of projective identification also results in significant changes in our conception of the dynamics of the transference and countertransference (Ogden 1979).

This inexhaustible dialectic imparts what Baranger and Baranger, following Pichon-Riviere, describe as a 'spiral' progression to the analytic process. For Bion (1970), too, the analyst's mental life and functioning are of central importance, albeit in a less saturated manner. In this connection, the following may be considered:

- the significance attached to the analyst's 'negative capability', a point tellingly taken up by Green (1993); by 'negative capability', Bion means the analyst's capacity to tolerate doubt and uncertainty in a non-persecutory Ps (cf. Ps↔D);
- the notion, so famous that it has now become a slogan, of functioning 'without memory or desire' (Faimberg 1989);
- the central importance of reverie as an entity that allows the (maternal and – why not? – paternal) α function to form α elements from β elements, and hence also of the analyst's activity in taking β elements upon itself and transforming them into α elements.

This relationship between β elements, the α function and α elements can of course be seen in primary relationships; it can be regarded as a modality active intrapsychically at all times; and it can be observed in the patient–analyst relationship in the present.

As a way out of this Bion-type dialectic, let me point out that a β element is deemed to be any proprioceptive or exteroceptive stimulus – that is to say, any sensory stimulus before its transformation, in the encounter with the 'α function', into a 'visual pictogram' that poetically syncretizes the sensory and proto-emotional experience of every instant of relationship with self and others. These α elements, when placed in sequence, form the 'contact barrier' that separates conscious from unconscious, but they too, when repressed, form the system *Ucs*, which is therefore consequent upon the relationship with the other (Bion 1962).

Any β elements that, for whatever reason, are not transformed into α, into visual images of the 'film' of thought, may meet with a variety of fates: they may be evacuated in the form of psychosomatic illness, thoughtless behaviour (characteropathic acting out) or hallucinations, or they may be preserved as 'undigested facts' (Bion 1962); it is precisely these 'undigested facts' in analysis that press for reception and transformation.

On the analyst's side, then, α elements are continuously being formed, and their sequence gives rise to the 'waking dream thought', which is always present, but with which the analyst comes directly into contact through his or her 'reveries' in the session – i.e. the images that suddenly arise and present the analyst with an unpredictable *Gestalt* of the analytic situation. This 'waking dream thought' is made up of a sequence of α elements that visually synthesize what is being mentalized.

I recall how a sudden image of a cemetery in a seemingly lifeless session enabled me to get in touch with a woman patient's suicidal fantasies; of course, this image had to be 'coupled' with the patient's text in order to become communicable (by way of a narrative derivative).

However, while 'waking dream thought' is operational at all times within the analyst, so too is it always at work in the patient. The patient has many sources of stimuli – not only 'undigested facts' and the transference, but also the sources originating from ourselves through our analytic approach, through the way we interpret or abstain, all of which are constantly renarrated to us by the patient. This is the level of communication on which I should like to focus (other obvious levels concern the transference as repetition, and fantasies as the projection of internal objects: Guignard 1996).

In this sense I agree with Bion that the patient is our 'best colleague', who at all times gives us our bearings if we take care, through 'listening to listening' (Faimberg 1996), to find a way of alphabetizing what comes from the patient and to facilitate transformation towards thinkability rather than causing persecution and evacuation.

Bion notes in *Cogitations* (1992, p. 64) that a painful experience may give rise to an α element representing a person rubbing his elbow or a tearful face; similarly, if one of my interpretations generates pain/rage/irritation, the resulting sequence of α elements might be:

A transfixing arrow	A roaring lion	A burnt arm

This sequence will remain out of reach (except through those rare visual flashes in which an α element is projected and 'seen' externally) unless we regard what patients are going to tell us as bound up with and relevant to their α sequence, in one of the many narrative dialects they may choose (which I have called 'narrative derivatives').

Pain/rage/irritation (arrow/roar/burn) may give rise to different narrations, which, however, will always have the same communicative value. For example:

- *A report from childhood*: 'I remember when Uncle Ettore took my tonsils out: I hit him and went on screaming for hours.'
- *A report from life in the outside world*: 'I saw something absolutely ghastly: a child was run over and his parents beat the driver to a bloody pulp.'
- *A report of sexual events*: 'It hurt me a lot to hear about the violent attack on a woman friend of mine and the rage and pain she suffered.'

Where our mode of working with the patient produces relief, well-being and feeding, the following sequence of α elements might arise:

A beach with an umbrella	A sea breeze	An ice cream

Moreover, this sequence could be narrated in various dialects:

- *A memory of childhood*: 'I remember the hot summers when Uncle Giovannino would come along and give us all some relief by taking us to the swimming pool.'
- *A report from life in the outside world*: 'What my father said to me cheered me up and relieved me, especially when he suggested we should go away together.'
- *A report of sexual events*: 'I was anxious about the exam, but Marina's hugs made me forget it all and we made love beautifully.'

Recalling what Freud said about creative writers, we may turn to any page of Calvino's *The Castle of Crossed Destinies* (1973) for a simple illustration of the foregoing. The margins of each page contain a sequence of pictograms (the only difference between them and the α elements of waking dream thought is that in Calvino they are preconstituted tarot figures, whereas α elements are 'constructed' in an original, personal way by every individual's mind). These pictograms may be likened to α elements and deemed unknowable if they are covered up; however, their 'narrative derivatives' can be apprehended on the written part of the page, which is a prose transcription of what the tarot sequence (α elements) syncretizes in the form of visual poetry.

At this point, however, even the characters entering the session can be deconstructed from their historical status – their status as internal objects – and become characters or affective holograms of the present psychoanalytic scene. I am of course considering only one level of the analytic scene: a character in the form of an affective hologram, from a different point of view, is obviously also a character-as-internal-object or a historical character. Between these three levels, there is in fact constant traffic, and this is the locus of the transformations of the internal world and history made possible by the here and now (Ferro 1992, 1996e).

This concept of a character as an affective hologram of the session adds the possibility of 'monitoring' the field to the analyst's classical instrumentarium. If we draw at the same time on our 'negative capability', this becomes a valuable aid to our work with the patient, enabling us to achieve ever greater emotional attunement or to recover this attunement whenever 'excessive caesuras' cause a fracture in communication. In my view, such fractures in communication are no less important than moments of 'shared experience' (Barale and Ferro 1992; Ferro 1999a).

Here now are some clinical illustrations.

Microtransformations in the session

These are unstable, reversible transformations that take place during the course of an analytic session and indicate the quality of the analyst–patient interaction and of the alphabetizations or dis-alphabetizations occurring. They are valuable signposts to how patients are receiving our interpretations and to the best approach for us to adopt in order to reach them and be together with them in unison.

Loss of . . . sight

A female patient said: 'My father has had a thrombosis in a retinal vein and lost part of his sight. But imagine: he wants to drive his car as if nothing has happened.'

What was this patient talking about? It was of course a real fact in the outside world and real people in that world. However, we may consider that she was also referring to the experience in her internal world in which an 'internal-object' father thought he could drive without having a clear view of the situation – the internal object being the 'precipitate' of historical and fantasy experiences. Another approach, in which the vertex of listening is in effect reversed, would be to say that the patient was using one of the many possible 'narremes' to point out to me that something had blocked my visual capacity and that I nevertheless thought I could go on driving the analysis.

This last view was the one I favoured; although I could have made it explicit, I abstained from doing so, 'working' instead inside myself on this communication from the emotional–linguistic field of the session until I 'found' what I had failed to see. I did not interpret all this, but took the first opportunity to put 'what I had failed to see' back into circulation. The patient did a lot of work on what I contributed as interpretation *in* (not *of*) the transference (Gibeault 1991) and said, at the end of a session a few days later: 'It's unbelievable, but I wanted to tell you that my father has completely recovered his sight, and now I feel perfectly calm when he is at the wheel!'

It has often been pointed out to me that it is not easy to determine the vertex from which I 'think' of the characters in the session: I glean them from a number of different vertices – real people, internal-object characters, or characters that constitute 'syncretic nodes' of emotional facts from the analytic field. The last of these is in fact my prevailing listening attitude; it turns the usual vertex upside down because, in my view, such a communication draws on the field and is a way of narrating its emotions – that is to say, it is a narrative derivative of the α elements formed by the patient.

If a patient's proto-emotions were of 'darkness', 'disorientation' and 'fear', they might give rise to a sequence of α elements such as:

A foggy night	A child alone in the woods	A ropeless mountaineer

This sequence could generate an infinite range of 'narrative derivatives', taken from the outside world, from fantasy, from childhood memories, from dreams, from anecdotes, etc., in one of the following modes:

- *A report from childhood*: 'I remember once, when I was a little girl in my uncle's car, how we suddenly ran into a fog bank, and he thought he could drive on even though the headlights were not working.'
- *A report of a dream*: 'I dreamt that I was blind and had a dog that was supposed to guide me, but it too had something wrong with its eyes.'
- *A report from life in the outside world*: 'In the surgery I saw a little boy who had been traumatized because he had lost his way on a scouts' outing when the guide carelessly went on ahead and left the group he was supposed to be leading behind.'
- *A report of sexual events*: 'While making love to Luigi, I found him so remote and absent that I felt as if I were plunging into the blackest pit of loneliness.'

In other words, the series of α elements making up the process of continuous formation of waking dream thought has an infinite number of *possible narrative derivatives*. The analyst must be a virtuoso in the upturning and deconstruction/

42

construction of vertices; he or she must take the patient's account: at face value; as transference; as fantasy; and as a 'narrative derivative' of the emotional experience that constantly forms α elements in the session.

Marcella's sickness

Marcella was a patient who had always overcathected the aspects of her life associated with work, study and professional competence, which she had pursued in an 'active', almost masculine way. When she decided after much hesitation to have a child, she had a dream in which she was taken into a kind of basement to give birth, where there were lots of men in labour on operating tables beside her. The dream can be seen as portraying the suffering aroused in the patient by the process of feminization in hand, in which more 'masculine' aspects of herself were being transformed into ones connected more with femininity – femininity in the sense, too, of receptivity and accessibility to emotion and the awareness of needs rather than discharging these in various forms of acting out as she had previously tended to do.

Once, very exceptionally, I had to ask Marcella if we could delay the following day's session by half an hour. Her reply was a brusque 'NO': it was impossible because of her own plans for that day, which she could not alter.

I agreed to let her come at the usual time in spite of the difficulty it caused me, and said to myself: 'How odd that she should refuse so emphatically.'

Next day, on arrival, the patient said that she could 'smell' everything very strongly. When I suggested that her sensitivity seemed to have increased, she agreed and brought a dream from the previous night: *I* had gone to *her* home for her analysis, but there were unpleasant smells of pee and pooh in the bathroom, which she could not get rid of. Then the plumbing was under excessive pressure, causing a crack to form, which had fortunately been mended by her mother. She went on to tell me about a film she had seen in which a killer murdered some psychiatrists who had done something wrong.

Thinking about this dream, I felt that I could immediately give a 'strong' interpretation: because her sensitivity to smells – but also to affective climates and emotions – had increased, she had portrayed in a dream the emotions generated by my request and her refusal: it was *I* who had to go along to *her* session at the usual time and place; she experienced her refusal as something that might have been unpleasant to me, even if she trusted me to find a way of dealing with the rage I might have felt, but at times she thought I might exact revenge and make her pay for it.

I was satisfied with this interpretation, which, I felt, opened up new pathways, but then Marcella telephoned just before the next session to say that she felt 'sick'. She came to the following session saying she was afraid of vomiting, and then withdrew into prolonged silences. After a few days, she described to me a scene from a thriller about someone who stabbed people to death. I could not help asking her whether her sickness, silence and fear of the knife were because she was afraid I might tell her things that might hurt her. 'Yes, "peculiar" things,' she said, coming more alive, 'like what you said about the dream the other day.'

I thought of a recent dinner invitation when I had been offered food that was very alien to me, which had left me feeling 'anxious', and I told her that one might sometimes have served up disagreeable things that made people feel sick or disgusted. From then on, dialogue with Marcella resumed in all its usual warmth.

Camilla's chocolate scales

Camilla dreamed that she went into a room where someone was going to spray deodorant to hide the smell of something to do with a lavatory handle on the other side of the wall. Then, when she touched a blue overcoat, scales formed; she tried to sweep them up and they flew into the air, but then they landed on the coat – they seemed to be of maize or chocolate.

Somewhat disconcerted by the dream, I asked the patient: 'What does this dream suggest to you?' She replied that the scales put her in mind of something she wanted to get rid of, but which came back again – something to do with relations with other people. Noticing that these words, when added to the account of the dream, gave form to something I had experienced with her, I said that, when she and I met, something immediately 'came together', making it possible to 'remove the scales' and have a 'good level of communication' – but then we had to start all over again.

'As if a passage had not been opened up once and for all,' she replied. 'Yes,' I added, 'but these scales are made of maize or chocolate.' Camilla answered: 'They are biodegradable, metabolizable.'

It was now possible to digest these scales, the heirs to the armour she had once worn, and to 'sweep them away, even if not yet once and for all'. I added: '– whereas the first part of the dream suggests to me that you are afraid of a deodorant being used to avoid confronting something unpleasant.' 'Yes,' said the patient, 'because . . .' and began to tell me something she had previously always left unsaid.

Narrations

These vignettes are intended to show how a transformational exchange can be initiated without strong interpretive caesuras, almost in the form of a conversational dialogue.

The absent character

A couple requested a consultation. A few days before the appointment, the wife telephoned to confirm it, but got the time and address wrong. On the agreed date, only the wife turned up: 'The problem is that my husband has had uncontrollable fits of rage for some time now.' Previously, she said, he had suffered from convulsions when he was under stress; these had given way to fainting and finally to these fits. Of course, I wondered who and where the 'husband' was. I said that she seemed to be describing a pressurized situation, like a pressure cooker that periodically 'exploded' if the relief valve failed to work.

'That's just how it is,' she said, adding that her 'husband' always expressed very strong, almost aggressive emotions: she had had a problem with the commas in something she was writing, and her husband always made a fuss about every comma. She went on to describe her English origins, her very controlled background, and some dramatic childhood experiences. I commented that there seemed to be an intense heat source under the pressure cooker, which generated many emotions that then invaded her. I asked if we could know anything about these emotions.

The patient now said she felt as if she had a high fever; she began to shiver with cold and to feel utterly shaken – as if she were having convulsions. I remarked that the temperature was rising, while thinking to myself: 'The husband is showing himself now' (in other words, the husband of the patient's narration was – in addition to her actual husband – an unknown part of herself, which was a flame of proto-emotions running through her veins like lava, although hitherto unknown).

Mauro and the bandit

Mauro was a boy of 13 whose parents asked for a consultation owing to their son's problems. I did not give them detailed information about how to reach me, and all three came along at the appointed time. I felt it appropriate to let them all talk together. They told me of their worries about Mauro's performance at school, which was barely adequate; they were anxious about the decision they had to take on the type of school he was to attend next year. He wanted to go to high school, but they were afraid he would not measure up and wanted to send him to vocational training school. I then asked to be left alone with Mauro, asking them to call for their son in half an hour.

Mauro appeared ill at ease and depressed. When I asked him if he shared his parents' concerns, he replied that he thought he could make it, even if only just. Notwithstanding my attempts to get a conversation under way, Mauro now seemed blocked, so I asked him if he wanted to use the sheets of paper lying on the table. He then readily drew a picture (Figure 4.1).

He himself remarked that it had just occurred to him that they had come by car from X and that he had had a dream that night: 'We were driving to our mountain chalet, where I like to go, but when we arrived we realized we had forgotten the keys, so we had to go back for them and return another time.'

I asked him if he was afraid that the time available to us for talking was not enough to allow him to get to grips with the problem and if he perhaps thought it might be useful to come back another time. Accepting this suggestion, he said he would indeed like to come again, and to come by car; he had already discussed this with his father. I agreed to this

Figure 4.1

plan, adding that we could use the time available to talk about anything that might occur to him. 'Yes, I'm thinking of a dream I had as a little boy: it was the story of a boy who was very fond of a wolf; when he had to move to town with his family, he had to leave the wolf behind, which hurt him very much and, worst of all, made him feel very lonely.'

Here was an initial unexpected key to the situation, provided that a way could be found of fertilizing the field, having reclaimed the soil by clearing away the stones (the anxieties blocking the process of communication), and allowing something to emerge. Mauro's concern was that there was not enough time. In particular, he was not sure that he possessed the tools necessary to begin communicating by opening the door 'of the chalet' – but then he found the key and the story of the wolf emerged. The wolf stood for the 'wild' parts of himself, which had been left in the woods 'for the sake of a quiet life', thus enabling him to live with a reasonable level of adaptation, but depriving him of the most vital and creative aspects of himself.

Therapy now seemed indicated to enable him to integrate these aspects of himself, whose absence impoverished his life.

Mauro arrived for the next session with an even clearer 'key' – an obvious desire to return ('My father was driving very fast on the motorway to Pavia'). He then told me the 'key' dream: he was with his father on the boat they kept moored at Z when along came some bandits with a pistol who started shooting at his father; he (Mauro) plunged into the water. I remarked that he seemed to have succeeded in saving himself, and that he must have been very afraid of the bandits. He replied that he liked a quiet life; he did not want to be a doctor (like his father) because doctors had to see dead bodies and blood, but would rather be a chemist with his own shop. Because this was a consultation, I avoided interpreting the fear of the violence that seemed to him to emanate from his own bandit parts (bandits in the sense both of violent criminals and of outlaws), or of conflicts that he was afraid might be so violent and 'fiery' that they might cause death and bloodshed. I commented that a chemist was less exposed to disease, death and blood. He said it was a quiet existence and just what he wanted. He liked animals: he had some hamsters and he liked rabbits; he wanted a dog and his mother would like a French poodle.

I suggested he might also like a bigger, stronger dog. I suggested: 'A labrador? Or perhaps you might also like a German Shepherd or a boxer?'

He now became animated and started talking about big dogs, from pit bull terriers to mastiffs, and said how happy he would be if he could have one.

We agreed to meet again to make a plan. When Mauro's father called for him, he told me that, since our first meeting, Mauro's marks at school had improved enormously, and that he was getting on very well with a boy who had begun to help him in his 'studies' once a week. So the decision had been made to embark on more demanding 'studies', and he had already been registered for high school.

The patient and the analyst's mind

My clinical illustrations could of course also be considered from other viewpoints, bound up with the patient's fantasies and history. In my proposed approach, the patient's communications are seen as signals in the field. The other vertices are also present and interact with my chosen one. The psychoanalyst's entire 'art' lies in knowing on which angle to focus, according to the needs of the moment, as in Escher's lithograph *Relativity*, which shows several different flights of stairs and possible routes – the locations of the infantile history, those of the internal world and the transgenerational field, and those of the present relationship in the present field.

Francesco and the damp, cold space

At the beginning of Francesco's session, the last of a difficult day, I felt like a soaking baby's nappy. I did my best to attend to the patient's communications and involve myself in them. The session, in which we worked on the need for a change in the setting involving the rescheduling of the fourth session of the week, seemed to go well.

The patient began the next session by reporting that, before coming in, he had parked his car in the courtyard below, not in his usual space, which was taken, but in one that was cold, damp, darker and in shadow. His little son had made a scene because he wanted his usual place in the sun, with a view of fields, but he had told him he could not have it. Francesco had scolded him because he had run away, but they had then made it up.

Having followed Francesco's account, I suggested that, although he had seemingly accepted the change of setting, it had actually bewildered him and made him feel sad. He 'responded': 'This room faces north; there is never any sunshine and not much light.' Immediately after my interpretation, then, he had formed a series of α elements, of which the communication was the narrative derivative. I now realized that I needed to look else-where, and I recalled the previous day's session, in which I had been 'soaking' and 'damp', so that his 'little-child' part had run away from a 'climate' it felt to have been inhospitable. I had preferred to give an interpretation based on the setting instead of 'acknowledging' the 'damp', 'cold' quality of my mental attitude, but the patient – if I would only listen to him – was quick to put me back on the right affective track: immediately after I remarked that I had indeed not been very welcoming, he said that the consulting room actually had an outlook on two sides, not only the north but also the south, where it was warm, light and sunny.

As an exercise, we could imagine that my feeling soaked and tired had generated the α elements of a damp forest and a sad child in the patient. On the following day, he had found a 'narrative coupling' for them in the story of the parking space and his son. My interpret-ation about the setting could be imagined as having generated the α elements of a 'radio that has gone wrong' and 'darkness', followed by the narrative derivative of the 'room facing north', and so on. The sequence of α elements of course constituted the waking dream thought, which was unknowable except through its – in this case narrative – derivatives.

Logically enough, the α element also draws on the internal world and the history, but of all the possible sources that which 'comes to mind' is the one that is significant with respect to the relational instant, just as the narration is taken from the external world but is coupled to the α element in such a way as to make it communicable.

Other approaches to the clinical sequence would highlight the characteristics of the internal-object mother and a repetition of certain aspects of the patient's emotional history with an insufficiently warm mother.

Clara and the voice on the answering machine

One Monday morning, just before Clara's session, I found a message on my answering machine in which a desperately anxious female voice was asking me to ring back immedi-ately because of a serious emergency. Unable to recognize the voice or to imagine who the caller was, I felt shaken.

The session began. It had a 'sparkling' beginning, in which Clara gave me lots of good 'news' about a number of situations of great concern to her. I did my best to attune myself to her emotionally and to be receptive, but was inexorably and continually distracted by other thoughts, to do with the telephone message: 'Who can it be, what does she want, how will I manage to track her down?' The session ended with the patient telling me how the suggestions she had made in a working group had not been accepted.

Arriving for her next session, Clara told me that there had been a 'freak wave': she had been involved in a dispute that had nothing to do with her, and her husband had wanted to break off a friendship owing to a misunderstanding. She had succeeded in making the situation explicit and calming the waters. She now brought some dreams: there was a skyscraper with glittering lights, but then she was in some underground caves, in the dark; she was a little girl, unable to find her daddy and mummy . . . and when she eventually did find them, they were somehow preoccupied. In another dream, she was teaching in a school; the children were not listening to her and she got angry; she realized that this was not out of any disregard for her, but . . . because they had to say hello to a disabled child who was passing. Even so, she decided to break off the lesson and leave. I was aware of the feelings aroused in a person who felt that she was not being listened to and that someone was not really there; from the joy of the skyscraper, she had plunged into sadness, gone underground, felt lost and alone – and then had come enormous rage. At first, I confined myself to grasping the emotions present in the room.

However, I appreciated the fact that she was able to negotiate these emotions, calm her husband down and prevent a friendship from being broken off.

The patient went on to say that at home her father too sometimes used to announce: 'I shall go away if you persist in not listening to me,' and that once, her brother, thinking he had been abandoned – forgotten – in a doctor's waiting room, had at a certain point got up and left.

I worked on the problem of being unable to control frustration, and the patient said that the main thing was not to give up: if only one kept trying, the door would surely be opened.

At length I felt that everything was sufficiently 'well cooked' for me to say that she might have felt that on Monday I had not been able to give her the attention she might have wished for. It might well be, she answered, that sometimes one perceived more than one consciously noticed, and what mattered then was not to let oneself be carried away by the feelings aroused.

To sum up: already during the Monday session, the patient had been aware in her waking dream thought of not having been listened to; the dreams elaborated and renarrated the transition from the happy beginning of the session to discouragement, the experience of abandonment and loneliness, and finally rage at my absent-mindedness; and finally, owing to the analyst's lapse, a precise description of what was happening in the present was given, but this also activated experiences from other times, which now came alive so that they could be worked through.

Other possible approaches might focus on the dysthymic aspects, the theme of containment/non-containment, and the capacity to respond to frustration in terms either of Clara's internal world or of the reconstruction of her history.

Igea: allergy and pollution

Igea's session began with her telling me about the happy, carefree holiday she had just had, meetings with nice people, and a new boyfriend with whom she had embarked on a relationship.

I was quite capable of 'keeping track' of her emotional movements until it suddenly occurred to me that after Igea's session, the next patient would be Marina, a woman with a severe psychotic transference. After a moment of distraction, I felt a wave of anxiety. Was I drifting away from Igea? To be honest, I felt that it was in fact anxiety about Marina that had arisen inside me. I then noticed that Igea was telling me about a problem she had had while on holiday: an *allergic reaction* to something unknown, which had given her erythema and blisters all over. Eventually she had needed 'first aid'. Then she recalled that she had often been called in to act as a translator: 'What is the Italian for "pollution"?'*

What had happened was a reversal of the flow of projective identifications: Igea was picking up my anxieties, by which she felt polluted and, through her narration, was telling me what was taking place between our minds. Alternatively, Marina could have been seen as a presence in the session originating from Igea – let us say, a split-off psychotic part of her – but I 'felt' that it was *I* who had introduced Marina into the session.

The situation could also have been seen in terms of invading internal objects, or the re-emergence of infantile – possibly sexual – traumatic experiences. However, my concern here is to draw attention to the interaction of the two psychic apparatuses in the session.

Let us now reflect on the above comment on the last three clinical illustrations, on the coexistence of other possible approaches to the material. I have no hesitation in adding that, in all three examples, I was able – after the event (*nachträglich*) – to discover the matrix of what had happened during the session in each patient's internal world and history, and I believe that this observation is at one and the same time both wholly and partially true (forgive the oxymoron). In the case of the 'soaking nappy', Francesco's mother had had three children one after another, so that she must inevitably have been a mother who was 'so soaked' that she was never available. With Clara, the 'voice on the answering machine' must surely have been a deposit left behind in my mind from previous sessions, a kind of ancient suffering in search of a 'thinker', for which I felt responsible – with the same responsibility as that of a mother, in Francesco's history, who was too young and paid too little heed to her son's needs. Finally, in Igea's case, the 'pollution' might have had to do with certain traumatic experiences in her infantile history, which thereby found a way of entering into the analysis.

However, let us not only take this 'comforting' view, according to which the analyst's inverted reverie is always a consequence of the patient's projective identifications or of the evacuation through the analyst of 'β elements' – or alternatively, as a Kleinian would say – of his 'attacks on his good objects'. I postulate that, beyond the retrospective use we may make of everything connected with the analytic field as a reference to the patient's internal world and history, there may be an inverted reverie of the analyst which the patient can

* Translator's note: this word is in English in the original.

50

draw attention to and often 'treat'. Just because the moments of inverted reverie (Ferro 2000a) may later prove useful for 'reactivating' traumatic experiences in the patient, this does not mean that we should forgo the possibility of in-depth investigation of the moments when the analyst's thought may – for reasons that have nothing to do with the patient – be in −K or Ps, or give rise to an inverted reverie.

In the section of Karen Blixen's *Out of Africa* (1937) entitled 'The roads of life', the author tells how, as a child, she was shown a picture, out of which she created a movie of her own. It was about a man woken up by the terrible noise of the breaking of a pond's dam, causing water and fishes to leak out through the breach. After stumbling repeatedly as he walks about in the dark, he stops the hole and goes back to bed. Next morning, in the light of day, he sees that the tracks left by his nocturnal wanderings and falls have traced the figure of a stork on the ground.

A retrospective look allows us to place what has happened in a tidy arrangement and gives us a sense of completion (as in the above three patients' stories). However, I suggest that the stork image should not be regarded as a full and final representation of the meaning, but that, in accordance with its nature, the bird should be seen as opening the way to new births and developments. After all, everything depends on the treatment we mete out to the stork – whether we kill it to see what it is carrying inside, or let it fly away, trusting that it will give birth to new life, and allowing that what it carried in its sling may sometimes be disturbing, if it reflects a dysfunction of the analyst's psychic apparatus.

In conclusion, I suggest that there consequently exists *a locus of formation of the image* (the α element) and *of the function that creates it* (the α function), and that great value attaches to this level. However, again as argued by Bion, we must also postulate the existence of a *second level*, namely that described by Bion as the '*apparatus for thinking thoughts*', made up of the Ps↔D oscillation and its associated anxieties and defences – of the constantly evolving relationship between ♀ and ♂ – and, I would add, between 'negative capability' (suspension of meaning) and the 'selected fact' (assignment of meaning). These are the loci where images are woven into stories and into the patient's history.

The following metaphor will help to clarify the situation. The patient comes along with a bottle of ink of varying size (his anxieties and proto-emotions, or, in the jargon, his β elements), which he pours on to the particular blotting paper that is the analyst's mind. I say 'particular' because, although it absorbs, it also gets soaked, and this 'soaking' can be accessed by the narrative 'nibs' of the analyst and of the patient, whereby the entities pressing for expression in the form of ink blots can be transformed into stories, narrations and constructions. In this way, what was previously a source of 'fouling' becomes thinkable, narratable and shareable. The microtransformations of the session gradually become significant transformations of the patient's internal objects and constitute a continuous rewriting of his history.

Clearly, in these processes the analyst's mind is necessarily one of the variables of the field – first, because it works differently every day, since the 'input' from the patient is only one of the elements with which the analyst's α function and 'apparatus for thinking thoughts' have to struggle; after all, the profound availability of the analyst's mind may vary according to how other emotionally significant situations have affected him or her (even if the analyst ought, given a sufficiently good analysis of his or her own, to be able to operate well 'on the average'); and second, because the patient's material may exceed the analyst's capacity for absorption and transformation if he or she becomes clogged up with it in one way or another – but that is one of the perfectly valid rules of the psychoanalytic game.

Other considerations might concern the *third fundamental locus* of the functioning of the human mind – namely, the famous 'royal road' of dreams.

Night dreams are very different from α elements because the former result from a sorting and filtering (re-dreaming) function applied to what has been 'filmed', alphabetized and stored constantly during waking life (Quinodoz 2001). At the end of each day, we in effect have myriads of α elements stored in various ways. There are then two possibilities: first, in the absence of meaningful sensory afferences, there may be an α meta-function, operating in this instance on the α elements and producing a syncretic narrative mosaic of emotionally salient facts, or, second, just as there is an *'apparatus for thinking thoughts'* (Bion 1962) that operates in waking life on thoughts once formed from α elements (an 'apparatus' described by Bion as made up of ♀ ♂ and Ps↔D), so there is an *'apparatus for dreaming dreams'*, which as it were acts on a second level on all the stored-up α elements and, in accordance with criteria of urgency, supplies a figurative narration that imparts meaning to experiences.

To this 'apparatus for dreaming dreams', which necessarily draws on the α elements collected, I would give the name *'narrative capacity of the mind in dreaming'*; resembling the function of a film director, it contrasts with the equally creative but instant-by-instant work of the camera operator who forms α elements.

It should now, I believe, be clear that much of our work is based on highly creative material produced by the patient: α elements, narrative derivatives of α elements in waking life, and highly sophisticated productions using α elements – that is, dreams. However, we also work with emotional turbulence, β elements, lies and evacuated thoughts.

5

THE WAKING DREAM AND NARRATIONS

I shall now consider in greater depth some of the matters already addressed in Chapter 4, which have always been a focus of my theoretical and clinical interest – namely, the waking dream, microtransformations in the session, and how to understand the characters appearing in the session.

Already in 1962, Bion wrote that the dream work with which we are familiar is only one small aspect of dreaming proper, which is in fact a continuous process that belongs to waking life, even if it is not normally observable. Whereas Freud used the term 'dream work' to denote the process whereby unconscious material, which would otherwise have been comprehensible, was transformed into a dream and which had to be undone in order to make the now incomprehensible dream understandable again (Freud 1933), Bion, for his part, considered that conscious material had to be subjected to dream work so as to make it amenable to storage and selection, and to transformation from Ps to D. He continued this line of thought in 1965 when he likened the role of dreams in mental life to that of the digestive processes for the body.

The second point (microtransformations in the session) was already one of Bion's central interests in *Transformations* (1965) and remained so throughout the Brazilian lectures (1973, 1974). He returned to this subject in one of his last papers, 'Evidence' (1976), one of the key questions in which is: 'How are we to communicate to a patient?' (p. 242). He invokes a kind of proto-sensitivity on the part of the analyst, in regard to how the analyst 'hears' that the patient 'has heard' his interpretations. This is where the analyst's capacity for attunement to the 'micrometry' of the session assumes fundamental importance.

It is only with hindsight that I realized how much I owe to Bion's thought in regard to the problem of 'characters' appearing in the session (Ferro 1992, 1994g, 1996e, 1998d, 1999a). Whereas I assumed my inspiration to have stemmed from my interest in recent developments in narratology (although that too is relevant), I must also have drawn profoundly on the Bion who composed that wonderful text *A Memoir of the Future* (Bion 1979b), which is so to speak a backlit reflection of his dialogue with Freud's mind (Baruzzi 1998). This work takes the form of a narrative with dialogues (reminiscent of that literary miracle *Finnegans Wake*), featuring Bion, Myself, Captain Bion, Albert Stegosaurus, Adolf Tyrannosaurus, pre-natal and post-natal personalities, and so on. Effectively, I seem to have adopted towards Bion what Green (1998) describes as the essential approach to Freud's oeuvre, delving in depth into his theory without any concern for orthodoxy, with the aim of finding the sources of pathways along which he himself did not proceed very far, but which remain valuable reference points for us.

However, let us take one thing at a time, recapitulating the theses of Chapter 4 with some slight changes of emphasis.

Bion provides us with a simple model of the mind that is susceptible of continuous expansion, as well as with the instruments for thinking, without actually telling us what we ought to think; moreover, these instruments constantly widen the field to whose exploration they are applied. Chief among them is the concept of reverie, which involves the existence of a constant emotional exchange within the analytic couple, in which proto-emotions and proto-sensations − i.e. β elements − are evacuated and received by a mind capable of transforming them and returning them in elaborated form, together with the 'method' of performing this operation. This entails the transformation of β into α elements, as well as the projection and introjection of the α function (i.e. of the method).

Another key point, as stated earlier, is the idea that dream thought (made up of the sequence of α elements) exists also in waking life. The dream discourse is thus widened enormously, for there is now not only *dreaming during sleep* but also a *waking mode of dreaming*. The latter, being a continuous process, also provides theoretical justification for the observation that the patient in a session also in a sense renarrates what is happening in the session itself. Waking dream thought remains inaccessible to us except through reverie (the vivid fantasies or daydreams sometimes produced by the analyst's mind from the patient's projective identifications) and 'visual flashes' (in which one frame from the ongoing film that records the process of dream thought is projected and 'seen' externally).

We can, however, know the 'narrative derivatives' of this film of α elements. Hence the narrative is a communicative derivative, involving minor or major distortions of what is constantly 'pictographed' in real time by the mind.

There are therefore two distinct loci in the study of the mind, and in the study of the mind in a relationship, as in the analyst's consulting room: first, the formation of the α element (the primal, unknowable pictogram), and, second, the narrative derivatives, which are to some extent bound to be present, albeit subject to different degrees of distortion, and which may adopt a wide variety of literary genres and pathways.

For example, if the proto-emotions – manifestations of sensory or emotional turbulence, which may also be due to an analytic interpretation – relate to an experience of unbearable pain, rage and revenge, the following α elements may be formed:

A crying child	A hurricane	A man firing a gun

These will remain inaccessible as such, but can be known through their narrative derivatives – say:

- *A memory of infancy*: 'I remember how the doctor hurt me when he removed my tonsils, how furious I felt inside, and how I hit him as soon as my hands were freed.' *Or*: 'I recall how some idiot gave me a bloody nose when I was a boy, and how I was so enraged that I slashed all four of his tyres.'
- *An anecdote from the outside world*: 'When his dog was run over by a hit-and-run driver, a young man chased after him on his motor-bike and beat him up.'
- *An account of a sexual episode*: 'My boyfriend tried to make love to me so brutally and out of the blue that I didn't want to see him for a week and I threw all his presents out of the window.'
- *An account of a film*: 'I saw a film in which a child was kidnapped and the father was so upset and furious that he managed to overcome the whole gang instead of letting them get away with their brutality.'
- *A dream*: 'I dreamed that bandits suddenly appeared among a peaceful Indian tribe and smashed everything to pieces – but when the warriors returned they were so enraged that they gave chase and massacred all the bandits.'

From this point of view, a dream could *also* be a narrative derivative of the α elements of the moment.

Let us return to the implications of this approach in relation to *night dreams*. During sleep, when afferences are at their minimum, the α function might well be working on its own contents, performing a secondary level of elaboration on the α elements stored up during the day, which are then added to the immense store of unused α elements (the continuous source of stimuli represented by 'undigested facts' – Bion 1962). This would constitute a process of 'rumination' applied to anything that required further digestion.

In addition, besides the 'apparatus for thinking thoughts', we might postulate an 'apparatus for dreaming dreams'.

In discussing night dreams, I find the metaphor of the film camera operator and the editor/director useful. The camera operator has been filming all day and producing α elements; at night, the editor/director takes over and puts the sequences of α elements together. There are two loci of poetry. The first, which I regard as the more complex and creative, is thus the formation of the individual α elements, in which the proto-emotional and the proto-sensory are transformed into images (an alternative metaphor might be a painter with an individual canvas); the second constitutes the placing of the canvases in sequence (only some of them; others are set aside), to form the 'exhibition', or night dream.

These poetic moments can be 'killed off' by interpreting (or decoding) the dream in accordance with a set technique or key, but can be turned to account by reverie, in which they are read in dreamlike fashion in such a way as to allow progressive expansion of their sense. Likewise, someone finding a kite might react in either of two ways: first, investigating its construction by taking it to pieces (this would be an attack on creativity) or, second, helping it to take flight (Duparc 1998; Guignard 1998). It is of course possible to describe its gyrations, features, colour and other characteristics while it is flying.

The first thing to be considered in relation to a dream is the kind of *reverie* it arouses in us if, on a particular day, we are able to make contact with our own waking dream thought. We may then be helped by what the patient tells us 'of' and 'about' the dream (i.e. the patient's own reveries about it), and we may encourage the patient to perform this 'redreaming' operation in real time. We must forget everything that belongs to our academic and theoretical knowledge, which must be literally set back to zero, to be redreamed if necessary should it come up in the particular situation as a new and unforeseen experience.

I should now like to move on to a different level – namely, the specifically *narrative* level (previously we were concerned with the α function, which is the capacity of the human mind to form the emotional pictograms, or α elements, that are its result). This second level has to do with what Bion calls the 'apparatus for thinking thoughts', which arises out of the Ps↔D oscillation, the relationship between ♀ and ♂, and the oscillation between 'negative capacity' and the 'selected fact'. The Ps↔D oscillation arises out of the mind's capacity to tolerate the fragmentary, the opening up of meaning, and indeterminacy on the one hand, and the closing of meaning – the caesura – on the other. Bion (1962) describes the growth of the container ♀ as a situation in which threads are woven into a fabric, the threads being made up of emotions that can then 'receive' contents. This in my view coincides with the analyst's capacity for relative abstention from interpretation, which allows the formation of the 'climate' able to promote budding of the contents (♂). If there is no growth of ♀, there is no 'place' in which to keep the ♂s. 'What I need now is a net to *hold* my emotions in,' a patient once said after a dream of bears emerging from a long period of hibernation. The oscillation between negative capability and the selected fact is analogous to the Ps↔D oscillation. At the same time, negative capability (Bion 1963; Green 1993) – i.e. the toleration of doubt and the opening up of meaning without feelings of persecution – is the prelude to the growth of ♀, while the 'selected fact' (the interpretation that constructively saturates the meaning) coincides with the formation of ♂.

When emotional turbulence bursts into the analyst's consulting room as a result of the 'undigested facts' of the patient's history (accumulated β elements) that are deposited in his internal world, the α function provides it with the possibility of first being woven into a fabric (α elements) and then of undergoing narrative transformation.

Some patients, especially those with narcissistic pathology, cannot tolerate something the analyst knows being made explicit.

After a session in which I had given explicit interpretations of content, a female patient began the next session by telling me how her husband had forced her to submit to anal intercourse and how this had humiliated her and made her cry. I imagine that she had experienced my interpretation too as a humiliating and tyrannical act. Similarly, after a session in which certain relational aspects were made explicit, the same patient told me about 'her husband's insulting phone calls' to her. From then on I simply had to establish a narrative 'attunement', in which the process of assigning meaning was shared, respecting the patient's manifest text and avoiding interventions liable to be experienced as a forcible entry into a container not yet able to receive seemingly intrusive and violent 'interpretations'.

I stayed with the text of the 'son left all by himself during the holidays and feeling anxious' (deliberately not interpreting the separation anxiety occasioned by the holidays), but picking up the 'child's anxiety at being left alone without his parents'. I stayed with the pain caused to the patient by a husband who did not want to spend his holidays with her (interpreting only the 'pain of not feeling loved') and leaving it to the shared narration to make a centripetal, initially very wide-ranging approach to the emotions involved, gradually homing in on them from the starting point of the patient's 'narremes'. There now appeared her friend Carlo, a kind man and a good listener, who could comfort her at difficult times, thereby also helping her to think more deeply because she did not feel persecuted.

Story-telling is thus a great 'metaphor . . . a process of metamorphosis. It constantly narrates the process of change, the transformation of figures that are modified by breaking down their own boundaries' (Rella 1999).

After only a few sessions, a hypochondriacal male patient dreamed that his bulb-like tumour was placed in a vase, in which – the temperature and humidity being to its liking – it started budding, giving rise to a prolific plant that produced one new branch after another. So, when the patient's inexpressible anxiety (the tumour, or accumulation of β elements) met with the analyst's capacity for assumption, metabolization and transformation, it turned into a narration of anxieties, fears and terror that began to be thinkable.

As a graphic renarration of the 'theory', I should now like to examine a clinical vignette in detail.

Camilla and the slight delay

When Camilla arrived for her session, there was a slight delay before I opened the door to her. Once inside, she said that she had told her husband on the phone that the medicine he had given her had made her feel better, but his response had been very cold, as if he had had other things on his mind; so, feeling hurt, she had said nothing to him.

I was tempted to give her an explicit transference interpretation: 'Perhaps you wanted to tell me something important, but I hurt you by my delay in opening the door and that made you change your mind.' But I abstained from doing so because I knew that such direct, unequivocal and explicit interpretations merely irritated Camilla. So I made an unsaturated comment about how painful it was when husbands were not available as one would like them to be. Meanwhile I found myself thinking about a friend of mine who had had a boating accident, and then about how, when I had told Camilla a few days earlier that I was going to be away for a week, she had had a series of psychosomatic reactions and denied any emotional response to my forthcoming absence. However, on the previous day we had unexpectedly been able to talk about the discomfort she had expressed through her body instead of by experiencing emotions. This was no doubt the 'medicine' that had made her feel better.

I now said: 'But sometimes husbands may seem not to be available because they are busy with something else; perhaps – who knows? – they are tidying up.' (The reason for my delay in opening the door actually was that I had been putting the chairs in the waiting room back into their proper positions after a group the night before, having not had time to do so until then.) Camilla's mood seemed to lift as she said:

> *Tidying up* – those are the magic words. That's what I wanted to tell you – last night's dream. Then you took your time opening the door to me, and I said to myself: '*He's not interested in me, he has other things on his mind, so I won't tell him the dream.*' But when you said 'tidying up', that cleared the block: the dream was actually that I arrived for my session and came in, but everything was in a mess, and then there was some-one else in the waiting room – a woman in a big bed, between the sheets, who told me to go away. She said she had to tidy up and I should come back later. I felt humiliated, furious and hurt.

I was now able to interpret the dream as referring to my forthcoming (one-week) absence, which made her feel excluded, and hence wounded and enraged, because she thought I was with another woman, or at any rate had other things on my mind, and I was able to show her how she also felt hurt whenever there was any delay in my response to her in the sessions or if my response lacked the warmth she craved; she would then also feel as if I was with another woman, deceiving her and leaving her outside the door.

A problem connected with an unexpected separation, then, had evidently initiated a sequence starting from the revelation of a blockage in the mourning process (with con-sequent somatization), continuing with the ability to talk about experiences previously denied, and culminating in the dream, which had metabolized the separation problem into primal-scene anxieties. This sequence was evident in our bipersonal field, in the way any 'lack of emotional response' hurt her intensely – precisely because it exposed her to violent feelings of jealousy, exclusion and rage.

Let me now attempt a post-session exercise of the kind Bion recommends for the analyst. My delay in opening the door might have activated a sequence of α elements along the following lines:

An oasis in the desert	An Eskimo in an igloo	A telephone with the wires cut

This would be an elaboration of the feelings with which the patient arrived (having felt understood in the previous session – her 'husband's medicine'), as well as of the new feelings due to my delay in opening the door (the cold reception) and the emotions that caused the communication to be cut off. I had then felt a need to disentangle this situation by decoding it in Kleinian style without a 'third dimension of solidity' or reverie, but I knew from experience that, for patients, being in unison is more important than learning a truth about themselves (often −K); today I am convinced that the growth of ♀ is achieved by way of micro-experiences of micro-being-in-O. My comment about 'husbands' had a deliberately wide and plural semantic halo, embracing the manifest account given to me, the reflection of the patient's internal world, the link and the 'mating' in the session. At this point my α function was activated, allowing me to engage in the series of reveries about my forthcoming week away, derived, let us say, from the formation of the following α elements:

A shipwreck	A rescue boat	A working telephone

which were dissolved in my unsaturated, narrative intervention. This gave rise to a process of 'digestion' in the session, allowing the night dream to emerge. The dream resulted from the nocturnal directorial function performed on all the α elements activated by the emotions connected with the problem of separation from myself and from her objects, both in the present and in her infantile history.

The waking dream (the sequence of α elements) and its 'narrative derivatives' are manifestly important in that they allow constant micrometric adjustment of the session. Of course, this does not mean that there must not be any caesuras, for caesuras and fractures in communication are the channel whereby 'undigested facts' enter the session and can be alphabetized: by monitoring the narrative derivatives of the α elements, we can 'stitch the meaning back together'.

The field, then, constantly sends out signals of its own functioning. We therefore need only be able to pick up these signals in order to modulate our interventions and thereby allow creative development of the field itself. The development of the field cannot be either linear or painless, occurring as it does by unforeseeable jumps and explosions. Yet I believe that *modulation* of the field is one of the analyst's main functions, even if the field to be modulated is by its nature discontinuous.

A particular characteristic of the analytic situation is the presence of the significant variable represented by the analyst's mind (Bion 1985). It is therefore impossible to refer to 'the patient' or the method without allowing for the fact that the psychoanalytic situation is determined jointly by the patient-analyst couple. Hence there are no empirical or objectivizable instruments that might facilitate a scientific approach; instead, the specificity of the psychoanalytic situation must be borne in mind. Without for the time being distinguishing between the various psychoanalytic models, I would say that all share the notion that 'unthinkable contents' expressed in symptoms, suffering or behaviour are transformed by the encounter with the analyst and his mind into describable emotions and thoughts, with the consequence of the disappearance or abatement of symptoms.

As I said at the beginning of this chapter, the science of narratology is potentially a very valuable instrument for us even though it is quite different from psychoanalysis. Narratology is based on the vicissitudes of the intersection of text and reader (initially it focused on the functioning of the text as such). It embraces a wide range of positions, from an extreme deconstructivism that stresses the 'power' of the reader on the one hand, to, on the other, respect for the rights of the text, without denying the importance of the subjective operations that all readers are bound to perform in their reading strategies (Eco 1979, 1990).

The psychoanalytic situation is of course much more complex, because there are two texts and two readers acting on living material engaged in an ongoing process of rewriting and transformation (Green 1973). Furthermore, psychoanalysis is a method of treating psychic suffering, in which the work of metabolizing the undigested residue of unsatisfactory or traumatic relational experiences is completed when satisfactory functioning is achieved – with the introjection of the method of dealing with proto-emotions and proto-thoughts. So although psychoanalysis is not a narratology but a therapeutic method that uses knowledge and emotional transformation, it must be recognized that the analyst's instruments extend also to the field investigated by semiotics and by narratology in particular.

Whatever the analyst's model, light is shed on worlds connected with the protagonists of the 'family romance', the 'internal objects' and the 'present relationship' between analyst and patient, as well as the characters who narrate all this. Analysis therefore involves a constant process of narrative weaving and reweaving, in which, according to the chosen model, the interpretations given may be strong, constituting caesuras, or unsaturated and open. In the latter case they assume a multivalent form that facilitates the narrative development of the theme pressing for expression in the patient – constructions or reconstructions of infantile, fantasied or relational scenarios or scenarios from the dyadic group field, which come alive in the analyst's consulting room.

Even more significant is how what has not yet been thought, or is not thinkable by the exchange and reception of proto-emotions, begins to 'press' to be pictographed (i.e. transformed into an image) and hence to achieve speakability through a 'narration'. In other words, the 'non-thinkable' becomes a shared account by way of a series of emotional vicissitudes whereby a name can be given to what was previously not representable. Naming progressively gives rise to the development – in the patient too – of the specific narrative quality of the waking mind (whether dreaming while awake or during sleep) that coincides with introjection of the analytic function. At a certain point, the shared narration is superseded by the active, stabilized function of an internal narrator able to confer a name, meaning and history on what had previously been exerting pressure in the form of emotional sensory 'lumps'. These specific operations of the internal narrator have much in common with the investigations and systematizations of narratology in recent years. These began with Umberto Eco's basic text *Lector in fabula* (1979), which laid the foundations for a semiotics of any narrative act, irrespective of its context, in the intersection between reader and text (or, in our case, of analyst and patient and/or of thought and thinker).

In one of his last contributions, Bion (1977, p. 235) recalls André Green drawing his attention to the quotation from Maurice Blanchot: 'La réponse est le malheur de la question' ('The answer is the bane of the question'). This is in line with Bion's notion (1970) that psychoanalysis is a probe that expands the field of its investigation, so that, the further we penetrate into the unconscious, the more work awaits us – unless we strive for a situation in which the 'revolutionary becomes respectable – a barrier against revolution' (Bion 1979a, p. 256).

Bion was wont to say that the reason why thought is so complex and difficult is that it is a new function of living material. In my view, this fear of thinking surely affects not only patients but analysts as well. That is no doubt why we sometimes see hypersaturated theories waiting only to be applied instead of open theories that allow the opening up of new meaning and new hypotheses: thinking is painful and dangerous, and entails a constant process of calling ourselves into question.

My chosen field, then, is a non-Kleinian Bion, who has studied his Freud thoroughly and constitutes a caesura relative to previous models of the mind (in particular, Klein's), and after a brief digression on certain points which I regard as of fundamental importance, I have taken you into my 'psychoanalytic research laboratory', a monastic entity comprising 'a patient, an analyst and a setting'.

6

'EVIDENCE': STARTING AGAIN
FROM BION

Some time ago, following a request from the journal of the Porto Alegre Psychoanalytical Society to write a commentary on 'Evidence' (Bion 1976), which I had not looked at for many years, I reread this contribution and was surprised to discover in it the Bion of whom I am fondest. In just a few highly condensed pages, he once again sets out the central themes of his thought and sows an abundance of seeds for possible future reflections.

The paper begins with a 'free association' by an analysand: ' "I remember my parents being at the top of a Y-shaped stair and I was there at the bottom . . . and . . ." That was all' (Bion 1976, p. 239).

Of course, this communication has a very wide semantic halo, and we could in turn play a 'psychoanalytic game' – as recommended by Bion himself for training the analyst's mind to operate from a number of different vertices – by imagining that the patient might be seeing his parents as high up and remote while he himself is a lowly figure beneath them. We could also see it as a transference communication, in which the analyst, perhaps idealized, is heard from on high, while the patient is down below, possibly fearing his contempt. Or the Y could be seen as referring to a 'zip fastener' and hence to the formation (opening) of a split or the approach to it (closure). Alternatively, the Y could be seen as reflecting a masculine genetic-affective heritage. The possibilities are endless, depending on how and where the statement is categorized within Bion's grid.

From my own preferred standpoint (Ferro 1998a, 1998b, 1999e), the communication could be regarded as a 'narrative derivative' of the sequence of α elements produced by the patient in his waking dream thought, which we could use to help us gain access to the underlying emotional truths conveyed by these α elements.

However, such considerations are less important than the way Bion approaches the clinical material: he in turn plays a game, giving free rein to a reverie allowing (for example) the patient's communication to be transformed from a visual to an auditory vertex ('Y-shaped stair' → 'why-shaped stare', in accordance with the identical pronunciation). In other words, he transforms visual into auditory α elements (and the corresponding 'narrative derivatives'). Bion the analyst is able to remain silent because he cannot produce 'any evidence', thus demonstrating (if a demonstration were at all necessary) the importance of the analyst's own negative capability – i.e. the capacity to remain in doubt, in a non-persecutory Ps until a new visual transformation takes place, into a Y-shaped entity that forms a cone or breast shape by pushing or pulling at the point of intersection.

Significantly, Bion is concerned that the interpretation to be given is formulated in such a way as to be understandable to the patient. Bion returns to this point, which I also see as central to any communication to a patient, in many of his seminars – as, for example, when he writes: 'you can't launch into a great explanation of the alimentary canal to a baby' (Bion 1975, p. 10).

Another important aspect is that, in his interpretations to the patient, Bion acknowledges and explicitly shares the patient's manifest text too; it serves as the 'excipient' necessary for the interpretation-as-an-active-factor to be accepted by the patient.

We can perform our own exercises on Bion's reverie and the ensuing interpretation (in addition to admiring the elasticity and creativity of his mind): for example, on how the patient experiences the analyst's mind as alternately receptive (cone-like) and held out (breast-like), or now 'drawn in' and now 'pointed', and so on. Bion, however, also considers the 'economic' problem (i.e. the benefit to the patient): the analysis can continue only if the patient finds it worth coming back next day, if we have succeeded in maintaining (or increasing) the patient's interest and curiosity. In other words, it is not a matter of an analyst with a 'moralistic' position, but of one who accepts being in the service of the patient and promoting genuine growth in him or her – based not on any charisma of psychoanalysis or of the analyst, but simply on a daily 'profit' accruing to the patient.

There are some other points to which I should also like to draw attention. First, Bion (1979a, p. 250) refers to the embryo's 'optic pits [and] auditory pits', which I regard, over and above his manifest description, as indicating how the analyst can extend his sensitivity and receptivity from the very first moments of each session and from the initial (session-by-session) formation of visual, auditory (and of course also gustatory, kinaesthetic and olfactory) α elements in his mind.

All this of course has to do with the possibility of 'recognition' of the patient's archaic mind through the knowledge and use of the equally archaic mind (and sensitivity) of the analyst. This follows from the conviction (which I fully share) that archaic vestiges remain in the mind of every human being, and are a frequent source of pathology in the absence of a sufficient capacity for 'alphabetization'.

A young male patient who had come for a consultation once started talking to me about his 'schizophrenic brother', whom I immediately recognized in the erythematous and des-quamated blotches evident on all the exposed parts of his body.

Bion now returns to the central problem of how 'to communicate to a patient' – of the analyst's 'forging his own language' (1976, p. 242). This reminds me of a BBC documentary about the American 'horse whisperer', Monty Roberts, who could quickly train any horse without the use of violence simply by finding the right way of 'communicating' with it by gesture. The documentary goes on to show how the 'classical' method of taming a wild horse entails violence and takes a long time. So Bion is as it were showing us – or helping us to learn from the seeds he has sown – that any analyst could be a Monty Roberts able to communicate with the most archaic parts of the patient's mind. In my view (Ferro 2000a), the way to do this is through the experiences of micro-'O' that lead to the growth of the container ($♀$), as well as to that of an α function of the patient's own.

The analyst's 'proto-sensitivity' is involved, too, in the way he or she 'hears' that the patient has 'heard' the interpretation; in this respect, the analyst's capacity for attunement to the 'micrometry' of the session assumes fundamental importance.

Bion's paper also includes references to Bacon, Kant and Plato, which I regard as 'collective myths' that can as such be shared and facilitate our being in 'O' in regard to what Bion tells us about moving up and down within the Grid. The same applies to the example of Picasso, the distinction between psycho-somatic and somato-psychic, and indeed to my own above clinical example.

Bion's concluding reflections on our 'feeble capacities for rational thought' (1976, p. 246) suggest a possible origin for autism or the autistic parts of the mind, in the destruction not only of the intolerable emotion but also of the very apparatus for alphabetizing emotions – that is, the rudiments of an α proto-function. Similar reflections on archaic states of mind could yield new ideas on the 'sense of guilt' and on what Bion calls 'sub-thalamic fear' (1976, pp. 245f.).

My aim here is to demonstrate how even the shortest of papers by Bion lends itself to an infinite number of observations and opens up an infinity of possible pathways. Deriving inspiration from Bion does not of course mean that we should become the custodians or defenders of his thought, but that we should make full use of the instruments he has given us – the seeds he has sown – so that we can proceed bravely (and certainly on the shoulders of Bion, Klein and Freud) along our path in the hope of tracing out new routes as well as, in particular, of opening up previously unthinkable mental continents – and, with them, new questions and doubts, so that we can 'emotionally' acknowledge the enormous scale of our ignorance. In other words, to paraphrase a remark in Bion's very last paper, 'Making the best of a bad job' (1979a), are we to use his authority as a barrier against the unknown?

I have also been asked why I have always been so interested in Bion and whether this might not be a limitation. The reason for my interest in Bion is that he has been a great source of inspiration to me on account of certain characteristics of his. 'We cannot call ourselves Bionians because so being essentially means being ourselves and being mentally free on our voyages of discovery' (Bion Talamo 1987). Bion has assisted me greatly in finding my own way and style of being an analyst, and I use some of his language either because it has helped me to think or because I consider many of his formulations to be still valuable for the development of thought.

Moreover, 'my' Bion is one who does not represent a linear development of Klein's thought, but who constitutes a 'strong caesura' in relation to the Kleinian model – a caesura that in fact gives rise to an entirely new and original model. One need only think of the profound differences between the notions of unconscious fantasy and of α elements or between the saturation and non-saturation of the respective models or of interpretation; the different conceptions of the unconscious; and the patient as the analyst's best colleague. (For a full discussion of these points, see Gaburri and Ferro 1988.)

However, at the risk of repeating myself in relation to central themes of this book, I wish to resist the temptation to drag Bion and his thought in one direction or another (to see whom he should belong to, whose heir he is, or who should be his heirs), and attempt instead, not to celebrate 'Bionian thought', but to work on the new horizons to which Bion's concepts may lead us – not because he himself intuited or proposed them, but because his model lends itself to this expansion and makes it possible. My position is thus post-Klein and post-Bion, while owing a debt to both Klein and Bion. In other words, I wish to emphasize the expansions of Bion's thought which that thought itself allows, whether they be linear or amount to quantum leaps.

The *first* expansion concerns waking dream thought and its central importance in the session. Alpha elements are constantly formed in the analyst's mind, and his or her reverie in the session can be seen as a fairly close derivative of them. However, the same is true of the patient. What the patient tells us, especially after a powerful stimulus – for instance, an interpretation of ours – can be seen as a *narrative derivative* of the patient's α element. In this way we can 'see' what the patient tells us as a continuous process of pictographing what is happening, or not happening, in the consulting room, thus providing us with a 'sonar' to help us navigate.

Waking dream thought thus permits continuous renarration of the session from an unknown vertex, through the *narrative derivatives* of the α element. If a female patient suddenly tells me she cannot understand why a little girl should say that the Eskimos live in poverty and wretchedness not only because of the cold but because they have no pipes to build factories, she is simply narrating the 'photograph' she has taken of a cold *session*, in which nothing is being created because the prerequisites (the pipes, or K and L links) for emotional exchanges (the growth of ♀ ♂) are lacking.

I come now to my *second* expansion. 'Interpretation' is not enough: what is needed is 'transformation'. In other words, it is not sufficient to interpret the fear of a cold, uncommunicative climate; instead, by working on the cold and the lack of communication inside himself, the analyst must 'transform' the climate and make it warm and communicative. The source of the 'cold' and the 'lack of communication' – whether it be in the analyst's mind or in the patient's projective identifications – is immaterial: the climate must be transformed by producing the 'pipes' needed for the factories in the session.

In my view, the concept of interpretation should be extended to any verbal or non-verbal intervention capable of generating transformations (Cancrini and Giordo 1995; Corrente 1992; Gaburri 1987, 1997; Hautmann 1977; Kernberg 1996; Lussana 1991; Mabilde 1993; Nissim Momigliano 1979; Riolo 1989; Rocha Barros 1994; Sarno 1994; Vallino Macciò 1998).

What I mean by a 'verbal or non-verbal intervention' is not only that transformation enters the field when something is expressed explicitly and in words, but also that the field is modified by a change in the depth of the analyst's listening and in his or her availability in regard to projective identifications (or, better, to the patient's emotional turbulence). As to these projective identifications, if we abandon our state of impermeability and become available for assumption and 'contagion', we generate a completely new and transformed *Gestalt*.

From another angle, an author whose theories in my view lend themselves to a similar process of expansion and who has much in common with 'my' Bion is Winnicott. In *Therapeutic Consultations in Child Psychiatry* (1971), for example, he anticipates the concept of the field, with its corollary of the assignment of equal weight to the mental life of the analyst (and hence also to his defensiveness) and of the patient in structuring the analyst's experience of the field. We also find the notion of a 'story' to be developed – even if for Winnicott it is a means of diagnosis, whereas in Bion it becomes 'the particular story that needs to be told' – and hence the development of the entire issue of interpretations along the Ps↔D axis (Ferro 1996e).

The concepts of the 'good-enough mother' and of 'holding' anticipate in more specifically mental terms (and in terms of mental functioning) Bion's formulation of the concept of 'reverie', the presence of the other's mind and of the environment as the other's mind, and the development of ♀ and of the α function. Winnicott's 'transitional area' encompasses everything that Bion places on Row C of the Grid (dreams, myths, etc.), and hence everything that relates to non-saturation and the growth of ♂ as needing an 'appropriate' situation – namely, the other's mind inhabited by emotions allowing development. Winnicott's 'play' becomes Bion's way of letting theories (or the protagonists of a session) combine and speak, as in *A Memoir of the Future* (Bion 1979b). Winnicott's 'true self' and 'false self' are analogous to Bion's notions of thought and lies. Again, Winnicott's (1974) conception of breakdown in many respects resembles Bion's (1966) idea of 'catastrophic change', or 'being in O'. Winnicott's (1947) article 'Hate in the countertransference', on the truth of the emotions in the analyst's mind and on the need for him to be able to tolerate them, is surely reminiscent of what Bion (1970) says in *Attention and Interpretation* concerning the work to be performed by the analyst's mind in order to bring about insight, while Winnicott's (1958) 'capacity to be alone' cannot but remind us of the 'negative capability' invoked by Bion. Again, Winnicott's abstention from compulsive interpretation and his reflection on the amount of change he prevented or delayed by his 'personal need to interpret' recall the concept of 'non-saturation', a 'story' to be told in order to be understood by the patient, work along Row C of the Grid, and the quality an interpretation must have if it is to bring about transformation (expansion in the field of meaning, myth and passion) (Bion 1963).

The aim of the above remarks is not to flatten Winnicott's thought or to hybridize it with Bion's, but to demonstrate the affinity between their concepts, even though they are expressed in different language, and to emphasize the importance of solving 'equations' and forming new mathematics. In so doing, it does not matter whether we use a notation involving x, y or q as an aid to thought. The important thing is that there shall be a thought in the process of constant expansion.

7

FROM THE TYRANNY OF THE SUPEREGO TO THE DEMOCRACY OF AFFECTS

The Transformational Passage through the Analyst's Mind

Definition of the superego

As we know, in considering the concepts of the superego and the ego ideal over the years, Freud vacillated between, on the one hand, regarding them as synonymous and, on the other, distinguishing clearly between them (Freud 1921, 1923, 1933). Grinberg and Grinberg (1978) emphasize the value of maintaining a distinction between the two concepts. In the classical description given by Freud himself (1923), the origins of the superego are stated to lie in the dissolution of the Oedipus complex, while its specific anxiety is deemed to stem from the fear of castration.

Klein (1928, 1945) investigated the early phases of superego formation, with their characteristic severity and cruelty due to the introjection of objects invested with the sadism resulting from the projection of the child's sadistic-oral and sadistic-anal impulses. The ego ideal, conversely, is attributed to the idealized internal objects corresponding to those on to which the child has projected good feelings and valued parts of the self, so that – in the normal situation – it performs functions of protection and stimulation.

However, the ego ideal may also be pathologically tyrannical, peremptorily insisting on the achievement of high and unattainable objectives. A pathological ego ideal of this kind not only gives rise to frustration but also exposes the subject to self-devaluation and narcissistic depression, as well as to the criticism and punishment of an implacable superego.

Meltzer (1967, 1973) introduces the concept of the 'superego ideal' to denote a structural relationship between the ego ideal and the superego, these two entities being regarded as different functions of internal objects engaged in a dialectical, evolving relationship. Primitive and inhibitory functions are devolved upon the superego, while the ego ideal represents the combined parent figure invested with positive and maturational functions (Mancia and Meltzer 1981).

Manfredi (1979) suggests that the one- or two-structure concept be replaced by a 'functionalist' position, in which the ego ideal, the superego and the superego ideal are seen as functions of an internal object, or of three internal objects, or of some internal object or other, these being recognizable and distinguishable from each other and from other functions of other objects or of the same object only in a given 'situation'. The 'situation' in this case is the psycho-analytic process, seen as a non-linear, spiraliform succession of introjections and 'projections' in which the ego ideal and the superego act as functions of objects whose characteristics – whether mildness or the imposition of malignant demands – change constantly in accordance with the qualities of the internal objects from which they have been exported by projective identification and with the time they have as it were spent in the analyst's internal world. I would add that the quality of the analyst's mind, too, cannot be deemed an invariable element of the process.

Bion's ideas on this subject are worthy of separate consideration – difficult though this may be – as they open the way to a truly relational approach to the problem of the superego. Chapter 27 of *Learning from Experience* (Bion 1962) is devoted to the concepts of the 'K link', $♀$, $♂$ and the growth of $♀$ and $♂$. Starting from Klein's description of projective identification, Bion abstracts the idea of a container into which an object is projected, and of the object, which he calls the 'contained', that can be projected into the container. If combined with or permeated by emotion, container and contained are transformed in a way commonly described as growth (Bion 1962, p. 90). The 'container' grows by the addition of 'threads' – i.e. emotions – that form its fabric (in my view, this process is mediated by repeated experiences of intimate contact, or 'micro-experiences of being in O'). Growth of the container is facilitated by the characteristics of the 'medium' in which the contained is suspended. The most suitable medium is the ability to tolerate doubt without feelings of persecution (negative capability).

It is essential to know which *emotions* encourage the growth of the container. Bion explicitly states that *the possibility of mental growth depends on 'the emotions suffusing the psyche'* (Bion 1962, p. 94, my emphasis), which constitute the connective tissue in which the elements of $♂$ (i.e. the contained) are set. The capacity to tolerate doubt and the sensation of the infinite constitute the essential connective tissue for the development of a link leading to knowledge (K). In other words, the quality of the emotions permeating the mother's (or analyst's) mind when he or she receives projections (or, better, projective identifications) is of fundamental importance. The capacity and quality of the maternal reverie (and that of the analyst) structure all future mental growth and hence also the development of a mature superego.

Bion then illustrates what happens if the receiving mind is pervaded not by positive emotions but by envy (i.e. in the case of a reversed reverie). In this situation (−K) the child has the sensation of a breast taking away the good elements he projects, so that, thus despoiled, he becomes the victim of nameless terror.

Bion defines this situation, which is the opposite of that of knowledge and growth, as $-(\female\,\male)$, which constitutes a 'particular type of superego' – that is, a superior object that asserts its superiority by finding fault with everything; it characteristically hates every new development of the personality as if it were a rival to be destroyed. In my view, $-(\female\,\male)$ has much in common with the 'abnormal superego' described by O'Shaughnessy (1999). The envious object $-(\female\,\male)$ involves an attempt to hold on to the power to arouse guilt as if this were an essential capability. All this can of course be seen as something of the patient's that previously belonged to the mother, but I believe that it may also belong to the analyst. The $-(\female\,\male)$ configuration destroys knowledge instead of promoting it, asserts the moral superiority and superior power of ignorance, stripping new and original ideas of their value so that the subject feels devalued by them. I consider that this risk is always run by an analyst who works with a hypersaturated model or whose mind is closed to the new.

Consider the following remark by a female patient:

> It feels completely different to go shopping with my mother, who is always on top of me, leaves me no space to breathe, and wants to decide on my behalf what suits me, or with my sister-in-law, who trusts my taste and critical sense and leaves me free to choose.

Although she was of course talking about a real fact in external reality and two different internal objects, I am certain that she was also describing two interpretive styles of the analyst, one of them more saturated and tending to impose a view and the other more open and respectful. This of course gives rise to a significant problem of technique: does the analyst interpret these two modalities exhaustively in transference terms, or, alternatively, can the analyst 'tolerate' learning from the patient the interpretive style most suited to that particular patient at that particular moment, and then transform his or her interpretive style and attitude in such a way that the analytic superego itself and the superego of the relational field uniting analyst and patient are transformed with them?

I therefore believe that what we call structures, too, are not 'things in themselves' but functions, or at least 'variable-geometry structures', which greatly depend on the qualities of the reverie, or reversed reverie, of the other to whom the subject is relating. Hence I would not take it for granted that the other's mind is always automatically receptive and available: the availability of the other is in fact quite often a mere two-dimensional sham.

Claudia and Old Ma Romina

A recurring character in the sessions of my patient Claudia was 'Old Ma Romina', who literally drove children mad, irrationally tormenting and criticizing them and sowing despair and anxiety around her; she would appear whenever the patient felt that what I saw as 'correct' interpretations were 'snapping at her heels' and exceeded the dose she could absorb and metabolize. If I interpreted along those lines, the level of persecution would increase still further, but I needed only to leave more breathing space and to interpret in a more tolerable, less saturated fashion for 'Old Ma Romina' to leave the stage and be replaced by 'the new teacher', a mature person with a good understanding of children, even if she insisted on their making an effort.

In other words, the superego – and the same of course applies to the ego ideal – can be thought of as a quality of the patient's mental functioning that varies with the functioning of the analyst's mind. The superego must be 'taken on board' by the analyst and transformed in his or her mind, partly through the analyst's capacity for interpretive modulation. It is very important not to mistake artefacts due to interpretive pressure for structures of the patient's own, even if the analyst might find it more comfortable to think in terms of 'structures' and 'problems' of the *patient*.

Some personal reflections

Before presenting my clinical material, I should like to mention some reflections arising out of my attempt to summarize aspects of the thought of Bion – of a Bion understood in strongly relational terms, who makes the encounter with the other the cornerstone of his approach (Borgogno 1999). This he does by extending the field of dreams to the waking state in the form of the α function, which is constantly called upon to metabolize afferent sensory and perceptual data (β elements): the success or failure of this operation is always as it were narrated 'live' by the patient, if only we know how to listen to it (Ferro 1999a, 1999e).

- Rather than speak of 'the patient', we should consider the patient together with the analyst and the analyst's theoretical model.
- Although the patient's 'structure' and internal world can be looked at, the 'intrapsychic' is bound to become relational as soon as the mere fantasy of an analysis comes into being.

- The analyst's mind and 'look' are not invariable or invariant elements of the emotional, linguistic and semantic field structured with the patient, but play an active part in its constitution. The analyst's mind is a variable not only in regard to what it 'receives from the patient', but also by virtue of its own characteristics and oscillations.
- Analysis involves a constant oscillation between transference (as repetition and fantasy) and relationship, the latter being the original and transform-ational entity that arises out of 'undigested facts' (β elements) (Bion 1962) and has the potential to be alphabetized in emotions and thoughts.
- Projective identifications, as Ps, are the engine of the analysis, in the sense that, beyond words, a continuous flow of β elements, or small quanta of projective identifications, normally travel from patient to analyst and are continuously transformed into the proto-visual elements of thought (α elements, or waking dream thought).
- Saturated interpretations of transference and content – which Guignard (1997, 1998) terms *interprétations-bouchon*, or 'stopper-interpretations' – are not the only instrument available to the analyst. I believe that, besides these, central importance attaches to interpretations 'in' the transference and to all the open, non-saturated, narrative interventions I have called 'weak' or narra-tive interpretations (Ambrosiano 1997; Andrade de Azevedo 1996; Badoni 1997; De León de Bernardi 1988; Eizirik 1996; Fonagy and Sandler 1995; Gibeault 1991).
- For long periods or at particular points in an analysis, sharing experience is more important than elucidating or decoding content. It is the capacity for being in unison, together with the analyst's negative capability, that allows the growth of ♀ (Bianchedi 1995; Bolognini 1997; Bonaminio 1993).
- The characters that come to life in the session, according to the vertex from which we consider them, have to do with real characters from the family romance, with characters corresponding to internal objects in the fantasy world, or with syncretic narrative nodes reflecting the vicissitudes of the here and now. Analyst and patient are often in a position to call themselves 'two authors in search of characters'.
- The extension of the dream world to the waking state ('waking dream thought') is surely the most important concept we owe to Bion; through its derivatives, through the 'budding' of images in the session, it constantly sup-plies us with the climatic parameters (temperature, heat and turbulence) of the field at any given time (Corrao 1981, 1991). If we know how to listen to it, it is a valuable indicator of the functioning of the analytic couple.
- I agree with Bion that the patient, at all times in all circumstances, is the best colleague we can possible have.
- My conception of the superego is as a model of a certain form of mental functioning, which is useful for understanding clinical facts.
- It follows from Bion's theory that what lies behind an over-rigid superego is

a deficiency of the function of reverie, in consequence of which many proto-emotions have remained unmetabolized. If the deficiency of reverie is extreme (extending to the point of reversal), the result is what Bion calls $-(\female\male)$. In such cases, all the mental operations that were lacking 'in the past' must be 'performed' in the session. Similar considerations of course apply to the dyad of idealization and persecution.

- I therefore seek to detect what lies upstream of the primitive superego or ego ideal, in terms, in particular, of relational deficiencies. This will enable me to show how the intrapsychic becomes the relational and hence to demonstrate the importance of the analyst's 'look' and of the passage through his or her mind, as well as the quality of the analyst's mental functioning and emotions, for every possible maturational transformation in the patient (Di Chiara 1985, 1992, 1997).

I now come to my three clinical sequences. The first demonstrates the transformations within a session at superego level, in accordance with the mode of interaction between the minds of the analyst and the patient. Although these are unstable, reversible microtransformations, they are the precursors of further possibilities of transformation. The second illustrates superego development over a longer period, in which relatively stable transformations can be discerned. The third reveals the long-term, ultimately stable and irreversible transformations brought about by analytic work, resulting from the microtransformations in the here and now of each individual session and from progressive stabilization over a period of time.

Microtransformations in the session: Daniela and the joint construction of a shared meaning

Daniela was a patient at an advanced stage of her analysis. She arrived for her Thursday session – between two holiday periods, Easter and May Day – and began by telling me in a very anxious, worried-sounding voice that she had not brought the money to pay my fees (it was the last session of the month): because she had the builders in at her own home, she had temporarily moved to her parents' house together with her husband and children, in a nearby small town, and had not been able to get the money to pay me.

She then brought three dreams. In the first, she was 'hugged' by Aurelio, an old flame who had rejected her; it was a warm, welcoming hug, and she at last felt wanted and accepted. In the second dream, two children were being severely thrashed by two unreliable mothers; she tried to take the children away, but when they wanted to stay with their mothers, she felt hurt because she thought they were bad mothers. In the third dream she finally succeeded, after all kinds of mishaps, in reaching the town where she was having analysis, which was a long way from where she lived.

Commenting on the dreams, she said that the first was really important: it was a new feeling to be wanted and accepted and to feel good the way she was. The second dream reminded her of children who became fond of their tormentor: she wanted to take them away with her, but they remained attached to something from the past. The third dream had to do with the organizational problems of coming along from even further away than usual, the way she had had to organize everything, and the satisfaction she had felt when she succeeded.

I interpreted that Aurelio might be the way she experienced me when she felt truly welcomed and accepted, but that at the same time she perhaps thought of me as a mother who ill-treated her children. She interrupted: I was surely right about Aurelio, but the second dream was more bound up with the experience of her first analysis and the relationship with her own mother – relationships in which she had constantly been told what she was doing wrong and how bad and inadequate she was; she still felt tied, like the ill-treated children to their mothers, to that way of thinking about herself, although she would really have liked to change her view of herself and her badness. She wondered whether I too could discern certain bad aspects of her but was keeping silent about them, or whether I did not see them that way.

I now enquired: 'As far as the delayed payment is concerned, what are the bad things I might be thinking about you? When you mentioned this to me, you seemed to be worried.'

> Well, that's easy: you might have been thinking that the delay in payment was an attack on the analysis, showing contempt or lack of appreciation of what you were doing for me – that it was a way of denying gratitude and destroying the link between us.

> Well, [I said] that would be a one-sided way of seeing you, overlooking all the trouble you must have taken to get here, all the organizing you had to do with the children, and all the miles you covered. Then there was a minority part of you that was very aware of the trouble you took and your ambivalence about coming, so that you arrived at a compromise: you came, but delayed paying me. I don't think that did any great harm: basically, Aurelio must hug all of you, including the bit that wanted to come and the bit that wanted to stay at home, as well as your having come but also making me pay a little 'tax' in the form of the delay. All in all, though, you managed to get here with very little harm done.

> But that's a new way of thinking for me. I'd like to be able to think like that more and more, even if some aspects of myself are still connected with the idea of guilt and badness, though this different way of thinking really lets me breathe and scent the air of freedom.

Medium-term transformations: Daria and the journey into the superego

Daria was a highly intelligent patient with a narcissistic structure, who was intolerant of transference interpretations for a long period of her analysis. Interpretations had to be 'non-saturated'; they had to take account of emotions in a generalized manner, without making the transference implications explicit. For instance, if a holiday separation was imminent, and she said that her son was anxious because he was going to be left by himself, she could accept an interpretation along the lines of: 'I suppose it can be painful for a child not to have his parents *beside him* any more and to feel lonely; and he might also feel excluded or abandoned' – but I could not then make the transference aspect explicit. Transference interpretations were experienced as accusations, and if I drew her attention to this, she would feel so persecuted that she would eventually skip sessions: 'I won't come to Pavia until I find my *mummy. . .*' The interpretations were in effect hijacked and became tormenting accusations.

I became aware that the nuns at her children's school were taking the stage more and more often; these nuns were anything but kind, but very demanding and critical, and would in general appear after an interpretation of mine that sounded 'critical' to the patient, although I had not intended it to be so. The tension would be relieved if I adopted a non-saturated, open style of interpretation again.

I began to wonder about the superego structure manifested in this way, which rejected 'relationships' just as the nuns did. Then, one day, in a session just before the holidays, the patient told me how her son had become curious about the nuns' enclosure at his school, had ventured into it and had succeeded in peering into Sister Gemma's room. She then immediately started talking about a patient of hers (she herself was a psychiatrist) who was delusional, felt loved neither by her parents nor by her husband, threatened suicide, and had witnessed the murder by a girl of her (the girl's) mother and sister. Someone on television had said it was very common for people to kill their children. I gave non-saturated interpretations such as: 'It sounds like the story of Medea, who killed her two children when abandoned by Jason – just imagine the despair and pain she must have felt at being left alone.' As we spoke, Daria went further and further, saying that she now understood her 'own patient' better and was no longer afraid of her. I decided not to interpret this game of 'Chinese boxes' explicitly, but to respect the levels offered to me, although I felt that what was portrayed as the *problem of the delusional patient* was in fact her own underlying problem.

I now commented that we had heard one story that had been closed off by a nun and her rigidity. A film could be made, I said, about everything that had not happened to the 'nun' on account of her decision to join an enclosed order; it would be about someone who felt unloved and unwanted and, as a result, was gripped by such despair, rage and jealousy that she would have liked to kill everyone, just like Medea, or rather like the *patient* she was treating, and whom she was no longer afraid of.

In the ensuing sessions, the patient unwittingly continued her 'inquisitive son's' reconnaissance of the nuns' cells, and each meeting with a new nun was followed by a description of another psychotic patient. I continued to narrate all this as another possible story about a nun walled up in her enclosure.

It now became clear that we were 'touring' the patient's persecutory delusional superego, composed of 'terrifying, walled-up proto-emotions' and bad objects. Only after the cells were revealed, with their content of unthinkable emotional stories that were gradually re-elaborated, did it become possible to open the enclosure, and with it a form of relationality that could be made explicit. There now emerged a more open and protective superego, like the one appearing in the 'new state school where the headmistress and teachers were prepared to listen to the children and speak to the parents' – just as I had been able to listen to the patient's infantile needs and to speak about them to her adult part.

Macrotransformations in time: Carlo and the long road towards affects

Carlo was a severely psychotic patient, whose prolonged analysis was marked by certain critical phases. A grandiose delusion had performed a self-containing function for a very long time, and its eventual crumbling was agonizing and all-consuming, in every way like a bereavement. The transition to shared reality was tellingly revealed by a dream in which someone was pushing him towards a precipice, or perhaps an unknown world. In the dream, Carlo saw a thoroughly ugly world, which was the world of reality, but when he viewed it through an opaque plate, it became much more attractive. For a long time, the plate had taken the form of a vision of himself, first as a Pharaoh, then as a Pope-to-be, and finally as a 'future Nobel prizewinner', a great scientist and envied scholar.

With the crumbling of the delusion, an 'ego ideal' so megalomanic that it was a source of persecution all by itself also collapsed.

In another dream, he was in an apartment of modest proportions (60 square metres) with a fireplace and a refrigerator, but this was terrible because it signified the loss of the palaces and castles that ought to have belonged to him. The grandiose ideas of wealth and celebrity were, precisely, the 'distorting' plate that sheltered him from the impact of reality. It was, he said, agonizingly painful to lose his illusions, to give up his expectations of glory and to become aware of his own limits, even if reality now seemed to him like a beautiful, desirable woman. He was frightened by the idea of emerging from a terrible world that was nevertheless exciting, and entering a world that was admittedly real, but also grey and banal. We realized that the 'plate' was a kind of Aladdin's lamp which he needed only to rub for its genie to offer him a world full of exalting stories.

Carlo's final emergence from the delusion constituted a 'catastrophic change' (Bion 1966) that occupied us for an extended period. He needed drugs – prescribed not by himself as in the past, but by a psychiatrist – to make the agonizing mental pain tolerable.

He dreamed of a nobleman's funeral, attended by peasants who had to work very hard. However, since Carlo was no longer the centre of the world, he did not now fear the derision of others, whom he had previously seen as interested only in spying on his every move. He could now reflect on the perversity of his 'sexual' relations and mode of 'relating' to others, which had always borne the stamp of oppression and humiliation of the other and had never been on terms of equality. He gradually began to re-own all the emotions that had previously been 'injected' into others and into the world, in the absence of a place to keep them. He accepted the prospect of a partial cure, and the inevitability of further years of intense suffering. Little by little, and always with great leaps forward and back, it became possible for his tender and affectionate parts to be recognized and find a place. A phobic area that made it difficult for him to move about in his home village remained, although the integration of sadistic and violent aspects was beginning to reclaim the surrounding territory.

The integration of Carlo's criminal parts and his abandonment of idealization were from now on accompanied by work on his superego, which was gradually investigated and transformed in his dreams. Having seen himself as a 'Pharaoh' at the height of his delusion, he now dreamed of two 'guinea-fowl' he had to look after.* They were suffering from a skin disease – which, he said, was the residue of his self-idealization – and he wondered what his real potential might be, as opposed to his dreams of glory. He felt hate, rage and envy towards me and still wanted to kill me for depriving him of his illusions.

He then began to ask for information about his neighbours; unlike the situation in the past, he did not *know* who they were (having previously seen them as people who hated and envied him), and he also discovered that he knew very little about me. He wanted to get to know me and learn who I was – in other words, he was taking back his projections and owning the projected emotions. However, as stated, he had a residual phobia that prevented him from walking through the streets of his village: he had after all sodomized all the women and possessed both mothers and daughters. He had admittedly done so only in fantasy, but was filled with appalling terror and guilt.

He dreamed of a 'court' that did not recognize the *legal principle that no one should be punished solely for his thoughts* and did not allow for his having acted only out of necessity because he did not 'know' any better; then he found himself before Torquemada's tribunal, which condemned the guilty to awful punishments and tortures; and finally a criminologist sentenced him to fifty years' jail. I told him that there seemed to be a residual 'lump' of his old structure that was not governed by the present-day legal system, in which the determinant of guilt was the *act*.

He now dreamed of a horse-riding teacher, and then of the childhood of the notorious murderer Pierre Rivière; he was afraid that an excessively good judge might mistake Pierre Rivière for the poet Petrarch. Guilt, if only for his fantasies, had to be experienced, suffered and worked through.

In another dream, which marked the beginning of an 'oedipal negotiation', he decided not to have sex with his 'uncle's wife', but only on condition that he could sodomize the female office staff.

Yet another dream portrayed Carlo in prison without trial. A lawyer told him to study closely the concept of legal responsibility. Beside him in prison was a burly wrestler. In the dream, he thought for the first time that he was not guilty of actual crimes, but instead the victim of a Pinochet-like persecutor. He then dreamed that he was drafting a legal document in which he asked the residents of his village to forgive him – in particular, for his abuse of women. When I told him that the most serious abuse was the one his megalomania had for so long practised on his affectionate and tender parts, he was moved. In yet another dream, he appeared first standing up, then sitting down, and then perhaps only less tall: 'resizing' was therefore possible.

---

* Translator's note: the Italian word for guinea-fowl translates literally as 'Pharaoh fowl'.

It later occurred to me that the delusion might have been an antidote to a pathological ego ideal and a tyrannical superego whereby proto-emotions were evacuated by constant 'transformations into hallucinosis', which invaded Carlo's world of violent and criminal emotions and thereby rendered it uninhabitable.

Then one morning, feeling that all his phobias had melted away, Carlo finally emerged into the streets of his village, meeting and hugging people he had not seen for twenty years and being fondly received by them. No longer afraid of other people and of the emotions that others inspired in him, he could now really move freely through the streets of his internal world. It was not long before he resumed contact with old friends and relations. His fear gone, he went to the 'Little Church of the Executioner' near his home and to the cemetery to visit his father's grave. He soon returned to a normal existence, fully in touch with reality, and replete with a 'new mental reality' that allowed him to plan his future working life and also to think of the end of his analysis.

Let me conclude by emphasizing that the presence of a powerful ideology in the analyst paralyses what Bion calls the 'negative capability' – that is, the ability to listen in a mental state of non-persecutory doubt whereby a new and unforeseen meaning can be structured. Failing this, the analyst performs transformations into hallucinosis on the patient, seeing in the patient's communications whatever the analyst's personal theory makes him or her see.

In my view, it is in fact impossible to work on the superego or ego ideal in a way that does not involve the analyst's capacity for reverie and the development of the capacity to think. This bears out Bion's hypothesis that the quality of the emotions constituting the fabric of $♀$ is of fundamental importance. If these are conducive to development, there is growth and transformation; but if the mind (including the analyst's mind) is imbued with negative emotions (envy, rage, hate, etc.), the projective identifications lead not to growth but to $-(♀ ♂)$. This is an anomaly in the functioning of projective identifications and reverie tantamount to a reversal of the flow of projective identifications which a functioning adult mind is capable of receiving and transforming, but which would devastate a patient with severe psychopathology, as it would a small child.

In other words, if projective identifications are not received and transformed, the result is the formation of $-(♀ ♂)$; an archaic superego comes into being as the adverse outcome of a malfunctioning primary relationship with an object incapable of reverie, together with an equally pathological ego ideal deployed as an antidote to persecution.

However, what do we actually do in analysis? A patient with this type of pathology needs the experience of an analyst who can receive $-(♀ ♂)$ and gradually detoxify it, in an environment imbued with a functioning capacity for reverie. The less the internal objects have benefited from the transformations brought about by the maternal and/or paternal reverie, the more archaic they will be. A critical point in an analysis is when the superego finds a narrative form in which it can show itself – e.g. through a judge, an examination or a trial

(Speziale Bagliacca 1998) – and finally be transformed without the need for 'interpretive caesuras'.

I have concentrated on what goes on 'inside' the analyst's consulting room because this is my, and our, specific environment – for if there is to be an analyst, there must also be a patient and a setting. However, it is possible to extrapolate from our analytic experience to the social field. Analysis and the social domain, for me, constitute two contrasting cultures, one of which I call the 'culture of reverie' and the other the 'culture of evacuation' (see Chapter 2).

8

SELF-ANALYSIS AND GRADIENTS OF FUNCTIONING IN THE ANALYST

The very interesting subject of self-analysis has in my view received less attention than it deserves. Let me begin by distinguishing the various senses in which the term 'self-analysis' is used.

There is an ongoing 'self-analysis' in which analysts engage as long as they are working with patients. There is nothing new about the idea that every patient can be regarded as belonging to an as-yet unexplored 'province' of analysts, who, for their part, are enriched and transformed by every patient with whom they work. For instance, I was able to 'penetrate' in depth into the concept of autism through my work with patients with significant autistic 'pockets'; as a result I was also able to re-own autistic aspects of my own which I had never had the opportunity of allowing space to express themselves, which had remained unrecognized and which could from then on potentially begin the process of transformation. This situation also made me aware that these pockets were much more extensive in my mind than I had ever supposed – until I recalled a childhood dream of mine in which I arrived by boat at a port in a certain town and saw the entire landscape as two-dimensional and lacking thickness, as if the buildings were mere façades like those of a film set.

Then there is the self-analysis that all analysts perform on their countertransference, including their way of metabolizing the projective identifications forced into them by every patient; this may extend to working on the analyst's reveries and acting out, as well as, in particular, on countertransference dreams.

These forms of self-analysis do not present any particular problems: the literature includes a plethora of contributions on such approaches, focusing to a greater or lesser extent on analysts' impossible neutrality and on their all-round emotional involvement (Jacobs 1999; Renik 1993, 1998; Smith 1999).

However, the aspect of analysts' self-analysis on which I wish to concentrate concerns not their day-to-day work, but analysts as human beings who have had an analysis and therefore possess a particular set of instruments for working with their own mind. This, of course, is a fundamental prerequisite for being genuinely available for working with patients.

It is debatable whether a truly 'transformational' self-analysis is possible, because transformation entails the metabolization of projective identifications and the progressive introjection of the method. However, it is my belief that, during the course of life, the 'circle' that every analysed mind ought to have introjected may become stuck, and self-analysis may then be the appropriate *method* of 'unsticking' the *method* already introjected. For this reason, I consider that self-analysis is substantially possible only for a mind that has already had the experience of an analysis. In this process, dreams are of course precious.

The analyst is actually an analyst when there is a patient with him or her in a setting; outside this configuration, the analyst is a person like anybody else, or at least like anybody else who has had an analysis. I am not saying that the fact of having had analysis confers any particular merit: it is like having needed a 'sanatorium' and 'streptomycin' for tuberculosis. A sufficiently healthy mind will have no need for analysis; analysis is a response – in most cases an appropriate one – to mental suffering. When one has had analysis, I believe that the process continues automatically for a long time afterwards, without conscious awareness of the elaborative work being performed day after day.

It is at times of suffering, blockage and emergency that the self-analytic capacity is activated. This is the situation I wish to discuss in this chapter, in which I shall mention certain situations when I have suffered mental anguish and how I was able to tackle them. A discussion with colleagues (P. Boccara and G. Riefolo, personal communication, 2000) led me to reflect on the concept of the 'wounded analyst'. In my view, the analyst has indeed been a 'wounded' person, but the analysis ought to have 'healed' him or her sufficiently. It seems to me that a certain 'tenderness' in the 'healed wounds' can be used as a working instrument, allowing 'harmonic resonance' with the patient's own wounds. Problems of course arise if the old wounds start bleeding again, or if new ones are opened.

That is where self-analysis comes in – although, of course, if the bleeding exceeds a certain threshold, analysts have an ethical obligation to undergo a further period of analysis, to ensure that they do not exacerbate their patients' pathology or have their patients treat *them*, which would constitute a perversion of analysis itself. All the same, this may occasionally happen in any analysis as an exceptional event that can in the limit be seen as having a physiological element.

The analyst as his own patient

At a difficult time of anxiety and worry due to a serious family problem of uncertain outcome, I was helped by a dream and a reverie.

In the dream there were two children, one of whom was well and the other very ill. I used my father's phonendoscope on the latter to draw out the liquid that was impeding his breathing. The dream helped me to focus on my concerns about something that might either come out all right or require some particular action – I did not know which way the situation might go. At a deeper level, it put me in touch with a very anxious part of myself, for which I needed to reactivate an analytic paternal function that could 'draw out' and hopefully transform something that was weighing me down.

The reverie helped me to look at my troubles with a smile, as one sometimes can. It featured a house with a huge elephant's foot poised above it: would the elephant squash the house underfoot or would the house be spared? In this way I at least managed to visualize my anxiety while waiting to learn the outcome of the problem that was troubling me.

At about the same time, I dreamed that I had a blister in my armpit, which came off revealing all my internal organs. These looked completely dried up, whereas my skin was taut and swollen. I immediately realized that I was 'swollen' with anxiety and all 'shrivelled up' inside, in a state of depressive debilitation that had sapped my vitality. Besides my work on the 'mourning' that was appropriate at this time, the 'cracking open' of my containing capacity was manifested, first, when I fell asleep in a session with a patient whose material was also depressive, and, second, in the – powerful and liberating – outbreak of a severe cold which both 'clogged' me up and at the same time enabled me to unblock myself. Next day came a dream in which I was to have an ECG, which, despite all my anxiety, proved normal and in fact revealed some 'suppressed wishes'.

The recovery of trust and the overcoming of the emergency were signalled by two dreams. In the first, I was attracted by a beautiful girl, for whom I gave up the 'study of medicine' that would have required me to be on duty on Saturdays and Sundays, and accepted the prospect of a less demanding job so that I could devote time to her. In the second, I realized that I already had a degree in medicine and that my wish to take some examinations at the university was due not to any wish to graduate – after all, I was already a doctor – but only to the pleasure of delving in depth into the practical side of matters that interested me. Following these dreams, I abandoned the idea of a series of working weekends and took a few days' peaceful holiday instead.

Self-analysis through one's supervisor

Sometimes it is the supervisor who can reactivate a supervisee's self-analytic function and allow her to do useful analytic work.

Stefania and Giulia

Stefania was a competent young analyst who, however, when her own patient Giulia had fearfully and hesitantly expressed her wish to have another baby, had stiffened up and found herself unavailable to the patient for duly 'receiving' this plan. Instead, she had allied herself with the aspects of the patient's functioning that opposed any change, and had also seen Giulia's plan as inconsistent with the development of her analysis.

In the next session, Giulia had brought a dream based on a book she had read, in which she was in a community of orthodox Jews whose orthodoxy verged on fanaticism, and in which she saw a picture at an exhibition depicting a crucified mother. I could not help pointing out to my young colleague that her stiffening up on the day before had generated the dream sequence: she had been seen as belonging to a fanatically orthodox community (the psychoanalytic community), and the motherhood plan had been 'crucified'. When I asked the reason for Stefania's stiffness, she replied – making contact with this situation as she told me about it – by describing a conflictual situation from her own past that had, without her realizing it, been echoed by the patient's plan, which had therefore met with hostility on her part. This led to a period of self-analysis, partly with me as its witness and catalyst and partly continued by the young analyst herself, until she found it possible to share harmoniously in her patient's plans and wishes.

Introjection of the narrator

I have shown elsewhere how an analysis can end when the patient introjects the capacity to weave every kind of experience one has with oneself, one's body, other people and life into a fabric of emotions and thoughts. This corresponds to the finding of 'solutions' in the strictest sense of the word – that is, to the breaking down of the invisible drama into possible narrations.

A patient nearing termination felt disorientated for a moment when her mobile phone became disconnected from its network, and she was furious with a male colleague who had discharged a female psychiatric patient whom she had tied to the bed. However, during the session, she realized all by herself how anxious she felt at the idea that she would soon no longer be connected to the 'network' of her analysis, and was then able to experience her rage at the prospect of being 'discharged' from the analytic couch, to which she had been so firmly tied for the last few years.

Transgenerationality

An aspect of self-analysis which basically continues the exploration of areas that could not be mapped during one's actual analysis is transgenerationality. Now a good analysis can, in my view, supply us with the equipment needed for exploration, rather than a fully detailed map of the areas to be explored. If this were not so, Bion's thesis of an unconscious in the process of constant expansion could not be accepted.

A transgenerational territory I have had occasion to explore by virtue of certain life contingencies is 'catastrophism'. Although I had never felt this to be an aspect of my daily life, it has nevertheless cast shadows at certain times. I came to see my 'catastrophism' as bound up with a fantasy of having to 'anticipate' every possible unforeseen event in case I were to lack the resources or 'presences' to help me at a difficult moment. It was as if 'anticipating' and 'foreseeing' every possible unforeseen event and misfortune would buy time and the trust that I would find a way of equipping myself to deal with the situation. It is like a poor swimmer who has been 'shipwrecked' and thereafter carries life-jackets and lifebuoys even when crossing a footbridge.

I realized that elements of catastrophism must have been transmitted to me by the experience of the mother of my maternal grandmother in the nineteenth century. Born of a noble but by no means wealthy family, which was therefore not equipped for survival, she had married a well-known musician, who had died suddenly, leaving his wife with seven very young children. My grandmother had been the youngest of these, and was surely marked by this 'catastrophic' experience, even if my great-grandmother had somehow managed to 'arrange' things and provide for all her children.

An aspect closely connected with the analyst's self-analytic capacity concerns the gradients of functioning of his or her mind.

At a difficult time due to worrying family problems, I was experiencing acute anxiety and confusion. I was managing to work well in supervisions, in which my 'experience' helped me, and I did not notice any falling off in my average efficiency; although less 'playful and creative', I succeeded in keeping up a good level of functioning. I could follow and understand the sense of what my patients said, but was aware that I had less internal availability and receptivity for their emotions and material; I was also picking up their 'response' to my state of inner pain. My situation could be likened to that of a woman with vaginitis or pelvic pain, who, while not declining sex with the partner she loved (♀ ♂), was aware of the difference in her receptive availability, as well as of the other's disappointment, dissatisfaction or irritation.

What is to be done in such a case? In an acute situation, there is nothing for it but to 'cancel' all sessions until the analyst is psychically 'cured'. It is harder to say what should be done in the event of chronic suffering, due, for example, to the painful life experiences to which analysts are as prone as anyone else. In these instances, the following are in my view important:

- The analyst should work to recover his or her equilibrium as far as possible.
- The analyst should try to 'metabolize' all the signals from the patient's text

85

in such a way as to avoid both self-disclosure and the risk of attributing something alien to the patient.

- With patients who are seriously ill – who will always be aware of the true state of our mental functioning – it might be more useful and genuine to mention that we are having a difficult time, perhaps through an interpretation, but, of course, without confessions concerning our lives or the source of our suffering.

Regarding the first point, first aid may be afforded by dreams, activated to mend the torn parts of our minds.

Many years ago, when a relative of mine was very ill with an uncertain prognosis, a remission of symptoms suggested the possibility of recovery, although this was not definite. At this time I had two dreams. In the first, I went for a check-up to the doctor, who told me that I had a tumour on my lung and that I had another six months or a year to live. On waking, I subjected this dream to further elaboration and then immediately had another, in which, having walked on to a big open space, I was attacked by a huge and terrible dog, but instead of biting and devouring me, it stopped a few inches away and calmed down, while I called a friend – a friend with a paternal function – who did not immediately answer.

At about the same time, a patient of mine told me that her husband had had his mobile phone switched off just when she needed him. She also brought a dream in which she was taking her child to a doctor, who might have been someone very dangerous and unreliable, perhaps a vivisectionist. Another dream depicted an aunt with whom she had never been able to communicate and a marriage that could not take place between a girl and a 'disturbed' boy.

Yet another patient arrived for her session in tears, saying that 'they are all crazy' at the place where she worked and that she would like to leave her job so as to get some peace and quiet.

In these cases there is no need for countertransference confessions (Renik 1999) – or, as I would prefer to put it, confessions concerning the analyst's emotional reality – and it is not difficult to perform non-saturated work on the patient's material and thereby to help the patient to work through it.

One of my patients, aware that my mental presence was reduced, told me of her sister's rage when she had gone to a seminar in another town and, arriving after quite a difficult journey, had discovered 'there was no one there', as the lecturer was 'off sick'; the rage was directed at the seminar organizers, who had failed to inform her of his 'absence'. Restored by this communication, which I easily interpreted to myself as reflecting my reduced mental presence, I gave active, judicious interpretations, after which the patient mentioned a friend she had met at a meeting, whose comments she had found interesting and vital.

It is once again Bion who informs us, in the Italian seminars (1985), that the patient is always aware of the 'quality' of our mental presence or absence, and that knowing this to be the case is one of the burdens entailed by the situation of being an analyst.

I should now like to consider abuse of the patient by the analyst. I am not referring to situations of extreme (often sexual) abuse due to non-observance of the rules of the setting, as described, for example, by Gabbard and Lester (1995) – situations where the analyst's self-disclosure leads to countertransference enactments or even to incredible cases of acting out. (Gabbard and Lester (1995) report the case of an analyst who allows a female patient with suicidal fantasies to sleep at his house, although of course in a separate bed; patient and analyst each wear their own pyjamas; the whole situation is ultimately reminiscent of a Woody Allen film.) I am thinking of the more subtle situations in which the analyst's mind is cluttered and less available than usual, so that the patient feels 'traumatized'.

For instance, after telling me that she had been through a week of personal and family problems that had reduced her mental availability for work, a young and capable analyst told me about a patient of hers who was furious with his own chief because, for a seriously oedematous patient whom my own patient had been treating effectively with diuretics, he had prescribed intravenous infusions of physiological solution, whose sodium content had exacerbated the oedemas. In other words, the patient was saying that it was up to the analysis and the analyst to 'relieve' the patient of his 'retentions' and the things weighing down on him, so that if the analyst too were cluttered, instead of performing a diuretic function he would ultimately increase the burden on the patient and make his oedemas worse.

However, can this be avoided? It is one thing to say that it 'ought' to be avoided, but another to acknowledge honestly that it 'cannot always be avoided'; it is of course a question of degree. Even Winnicott refers to the 'good enough' mother, and the analyst too can aspire only to be 'good enough'. Provided that analysts can recognize their own dysfunctional moments and apply the appropriate remedy, elaboration of the countertransference, a piece of concentrated self-analysis or a dream or series of dreams often suffice for the recovery of 'good enough' mental functioning. If these remedies prove inadequate, it is incumbent on analysts to seek help for the 'metabolization' of whatever is cluttering their mind at their point in their professional, family or personal life. In many psychoanalytic societies, it is considered normal and desirable, and is indeed taken for granted, that even an expert, famous analyst may have one or more periods of reanalysis during the course of his or her career – as, incidentally, Freud recommended. What matters most in my opinion is for us to acknowledge fully that the analyst's mental functioning is a significant variable of the field.

Another risk to which analysts are exposed is idealization of their own theory and technique. This may constitute an abuse whenever, as stated in previous chapters, it is superimposed on respectful listening to what their patients say. Moreover, those patients are certainly not there to treat us or to concern themselves with our mind, but are, as Bion puts it, our 'best colleague' – or our 'secret sharer', in the words of Conrad as quoted by Gaburri (1986). And, if we know how to listen to them, our patients also become valued teachers of technique: as Willy Baranger used to say, Freud's greatest merit was that he 'listened' to his patients.

In this connection, I reproduce here part of a session with a young male patient of mine. It is a session reviewed after a lapse of some years, in accordance with what is now my usual custom, to see what changes in theory and technique I have 'made my own' in the interim. The patient was Piero, a psychotic adolescent.

Piero

Piero rings the bell several times.

Patient   Did you see how I rang?

Analyst   Like a member of the family who is in a hurry to arrive.

Patient   Well, I suppose I *am* now a member of the family . . . I'll tell you right away that I am afraid [meanwhile he is eating sweets] that everything is filthy with 'S' and 'Sh' – absolutely everything – and that's why I am not sitting down: the ground seems to me like 'Sh'.

Analyst   And maybe you're afraid that the whole world is 'shit', that all relationships are filthy, including this one. Insincere.

Patient   Yes, surely, but not so fast, otherwise I'll get angry. You should tell me these things, but calmly, one at a time, without rush, one thing at a time, otherwise I'll get angry. In fact I've already got angry – I must call you a prick and a stupid bugger, or else I won't have any peace.

Analyst   Maybe you want me to learn to be at your side without rushing; then you can trust me.

Patient   Now I'll tell you something else that is tormenting me, but you mustn't laugh. I'm afraid that when my dad goes to the loo, he doesn't wash his hands or wipe his bum, and that he does it on the floor and makes everything filthy.

Analyst   And perhaps you're afraid that not only your dad but I too might be a filthy person, but filthy inside as well.

Patient   And . . . a scumbag, crude and crazy! Now I've said it.

Analyst   I wonder if, when you are worried and afraid that I might be crazy, you are thinking of the things I might sometimes say – things I say in a hurry, without having thought enough about them, like, for example . . .

88

Patient Speed limit 60 kilometres an hour . . . You've already said enough, but slow down . . .

Analyst Well, you seem to me to be like a cop, but a tolerant one.

Patient Isn't it true that I'm helping you?

Analyst I think it is true, and also that you are helping us keep our speed under control.

Patient I understand everything perfectly well, but I need time and breaks. Oh! My tooth [moving the sweets about in his mouth]: look how it moves!

Analyst [laughing] Well, you seem like a boy making jokes affectionately with his dad.

Patient But look, something else is tormenting me, I must tell you, I'm jealous. I'm thinking of that black-haired woman patient, whom I expect you find nice and clean, not like me, and then I'm thinking of my sister's meeting with the psychologist.

Analyst These thoughts make you suffer, perhaps because they involve exclusion and you're afraid I might have other preferences.

Patient And that I might be worth no more than 'Sh' to you, quite worthless; well, I'd like a machine gun.

Analyst These thoughts of mine have made you angry; perhaps you also thought it is a long time till Monday.

Patient But do you know what I've discovered? That my grandmother's husband was a Sicilian.

Analyst Maybe we have something else in common, apart from the high-necked sweater. [Piero puts down his sweet papers.] I wonder if you too are afraid of making this room filthy . . .

Patient Not filthy, it's only paper; I am afraid my father does it with shit.

Analyst Now I've said something else that won't do.

Patient Oh! [relieved] Well, now I understand, perhaps what you say is true, but it's very quick.

Analyst I can't help disturbing you with what I say, but it's important for it to be bearable.

Patient Well, anyway, it's a long time till Monday; I shan't get angry, but I'll miss you.

In this session the patient has surely given me an extraordinary lesson in interpretive technique, which I had at the time been only partly able to 'make my own'. He was telling me, in substance, that the analyst's mind must operate first of all in a 'receiving' and 'containing' manner and that interpretive pressure excessively oriented towards rendering the relationship explicit makes everything 'filthy' and generates anxiety rather than giving relief. However, as soon as I failed to pick up his 'movement' – his loose milk teeth – the result was an immediate fracture that needed to be 'cleared up'; and another fracture occurred when, as a '(Sicilian) bully', I drew attention to the weekend separation instead of looking at the fracture in our communication.

Again, there are two aspects to every psychotic pathology. First, the α function (i.e. the 'method' of generating α elements that ought to have been transmitted by a good maternal/paternal reverie) is deficient. Second, there is a deficiency in the growth of $\female$, so that the patients are exposed to excess pressure from β

elements and emotional proto-contents (♂); the patients therefore do not need further emotional stimuli, but instead to feel that their anxieties have been received and held, so that they can have experiences of being received (♀) that they will then be able to introject as ways of containing their emotional pressures. Moreover, the products of the α function must be kept in the analyst's mind for a long time before they can be shared in such a way and at such a time as the patients will eventually indicate.

A female supervisee was telling me about the case of a homosexual boy whom she described right away as 'feeble, inexpressive and sanctimonious' and who, from their very first meetings, had talked about his passion for 'violent macho films'; immediately after, he had gone on to describe his fantasy of 'fellatio'. Not 'daring' to take the path of violence, of the uncontainable penetrating fantasy and 'fellatio', as a way of managing an uncontainable 'Charles Bronson', the therapist had instead adopted the pacifying approach of equating penis and nipple and mixing up semen and milk. In this way she had used theory to keep at bay the uncontainable Charles Bronson, Genghis Khan, King Kong or what have you, which had again sought expression through the patient's phobia of weapons.

Some months later, therapist and patient found themselves blanketed in a climate of boredom, in which the patient would describe his day, telling how he was studying 'civil law' and how he did not play football: instead of going on to the pitch, he would sit on a bench and keep a record of the proceedings. Once again, the therapist failed to pick up these communications as reflecting what was going on in the sessions – how the boredom was a kind of sleeping pill administered to violent proto-emotions felt to be unmanageable. She also did not realize that the patient was describing the sessions as something in which he was 'sitting on a bench, off the pitch, just keeping a record'. And she missed the patient's only flash of life, which came when he described his passion for a rock singer whose speciality was songs of protest and hate.

The association aroused in me by this therapy was to Marie Belloc Lowndes's book *The Lodger* (1913), in which an English family in straitened circumstances let a room to a tenant who, amidst a dull and drowsy atmosphere, turns out to be Jack the Ripper. When I conveyed this interpretation to my supervisee, she was petrified: she admitted to a terrible fear of violence and to an aversion to violent films and books.

So the presence of a 'blind spot', or 'no-go area', in the therapist's mind also blocked the way to all the other stories the patient was – unwittingly – waiting to tell. After the supervision, when my colleague had mentally moved on to a different wavelength, the patient said he had been to the cinema and 'seen' *Hannibal*.

9

PIVOTAL-AGE CRISES AND PIVOTAL-EVENT CRISES

I use the term 'pivotal-age crises' to describe the common features observed in the transitions between increasingly complex significant age bands. Specifically, we can distinguish the crisis of adolescence, the mid-life crisis, the crisis of the third age and the fourth-age crisis. The prolongation of average life span has in my view at least doubled the number of these pivotal points in life.

An aspect shared by all these transitions is the element of 'catastrophic change' (Bion 1966), with the coexistence of mourning for what has been lost, openness to the new, and the capacity to metabolize the emotions aroused. In other words, the autistic nuclei that are usually spread over a person's existential routine, the capacity for mourning and the ability to find a place for the new and its meanings are all put to the test.

Each of these pivotal moments of course has its own peculiarities and characteristics, in addition to the common features mentioned. Moreover, each is in my view more complex than its predecessor because each brings one closer to the final pivotal point – namely death.

I recall that, on the eve of my fortieth birthday, I dreamed that I went to the station to buy a railway ticket and offered the booking clerk the silver paper from a bar of chocolate: in my mind, I was already visualizing the Silver Card issued to 60-year-olds in Italy.

Whereas in the past attention focused on one pivotal crisis only – the mid-life crisis (as brilliantly described by Elliott Jaques in 1965) – it now seems to me that such a crisis occurs every ten years from the age of 40 on; that at least is the impression I have gained from quite a few patients, as well as myself. At these existential turning points, every individual's entire constellation of anxieties and defences is activated, and a wide range of solutions and outcomes are of course possible – some complex, some radical and some involving compromise. We observe manic passions in youth, often with painful sequelae, or denial and postponement of the problem. We may also see an acceptance of temporality in the form of a 'nostalgic journey' whereby the problem is worked through. A useful vaccine is in my opinion dreaming and the avoidance of acting out.

It is interesting to consider the vast number of literary works, films, plays and paintings that narrate and renarrate pivotal-age problems, which are treated from a wide variety of angles and provided with different solutions. Risking the charge of arbitrariness, we could contemplate such artistic creations as if they were *case histories*, telling as they do of the degree of success or failure of these mourning operations, or of the possible defences deployed in an attempt to circumvent – at least mentally – these inescapable problems. For me, for now at least, the two extremes are, on the one hand, Bergman's *Wild Strawberries* (1957), which I see as a successful solution to the problems raised and only partially solved in *The Seventh Seal* (1956), and, on the other, *The Blue Angel* (1930), which illustrates a vain, desperate, manic and paranoid attempt to flee from time and its constraints. *Wild Strawberries* may be said to demonstrate from the beginning the centrality of the problem of time through the hero's dream of the handless clock and of his own funeral.

For a basic overview, we could track with the camera of our mind's eye from *The Blue Angel* (the original novel by Heinrich Mann is even finer than the excellent film), via Fritz Lang's *The Woman in the Window* (1944), Oscar Wilde's *The Picture of Dorian Gray*, Edgar Allan Poe's 'The Facts in the Case of M. Valdemar', Italo Svevo's *As a Man Grows Older* and August Strindberg's *Alone*, to several of the works of Henrik Ibsen. However, I must stop now because I realize that there is not a single novelist, playwright or film director who has not tackled this subject.

To return to my subject, I shall now illustrate the emotions, passions and transformations instigated by certain situations that I have had occasion to witness.

Mario

Mario was a 50-year-old engineer who had already had an analysis, which had enabled him to stabilize his emotional life and to mitigate a fairly serious narcissistic personality that had made his relationships unstable. He had married during his analysis and subsequently had three children. He worked at a European Television Research Centre in the French town where he also lived. A few years after the end of his analysis, I received an alarming telephone call from Mario, who was obviously in crisis, asking for an appointment. He was afraid that he had fallen in love with a young laboratory technician with whom he worked side by side – 'elbow to elbow'. I felt that this phrase of Mario's was significant because it reminded me of another, 'bending the elbow', which he used to describe the infrequent but violent drunken binges in which he indulged to avoid mental pain and depression.

Given that he would have to come from France and that he was not prepared to consult a French colleague, Mario and I decided that we would see each other once a month for two consecutive hours. Relevant aspects are not only the sequence of dreams brought by Mario, which extended from 'contagion' (!) to 'cure', but also, in particular, his written notes, some of them set down when the crisis began and illustrating his attempts at self-analysis, and others made subsequently for me to read.

Mario recalled a disturbing fantasy he had had the first time he had been with Françoise at a brasserie during a work break: 'I looked at her prominent, throbbing jugular.' He himself had been struck by the vampiric element of his fantasy – the vampire's need to be out of time and to quench his thirst with 'fresh, young blood'. According to his notes, he had thought not only of Dracula but also of Faust and his pact with the Devil.

He then dreamed that he was lost in an unknown town; not only could he not find the hotel where his wife and children were staying, but also he could not even remember its name. However, he met a coachman who spoke his language and who he hoped would be able to help him. So he had got lost; he had lost his bearings, forgetting his wife and children, or at least their 'place', but a self-analytic capacity – a paternal function – remained watchful.

Another dream followed, in which he seemed to find his wife and children again and remembered how certain friends had negotiated the mid-life crisis in various ways. Yet Mario's continence did not last long, and he could not prevent himself from going off at a tangent, as another dream indicated: 'First of all I was in a toy plane/torpedo/motor/torpedo-boat travelling through subterranean channels, but I knew the way and it was safe and enjoyable.' All of a sudden something snapped, and a new, unexpected road opened up. The toy torpedo had access to it and a new, strange tool was discovered: a kind of rotating drill that could open up new roads as it moved forward, outside of the channels he knew. In the dream, Mario felt fascination, but also fear – 'fear of adventure, fear of getting cut off . . . of not being able to turn back'. He then tried to go into reverse after starting up the drill: 'It's possible . . .' Mario did not know what to do: he was afraid of venturing into unknown territory, but fascinated by the new prospects. The situation was potentially explosive and the forces at work were violent; a degree of mania was already in evidence, but the sense of danger held him back.

Meanwhile the temperature of the dreams rose, and at the same time his meetings with Françoise aroused long-forgotten feelings and emotions. He studied her every word and gesture; every sentence became a source of possible promises or great suffering. Why did Françoise blush when telling him about something personal? And why did she lower her eyes in embarrassment when talking about the crisis with her boyfriend, with whom she was about to split up? Were these signs of interest and availability?

He imagined a story with Françoise; he realized that he would have liked to relive his last fifteen years, get married and have little children. His own were now grown up and going their own way. He understood that this would be a self-deception and that time was nevertheless passing.

Mario had a dream in which some people showed him how wine was made; he trusted them . . . so many bottles . . . Mario lost his head. He decided to confess his love to

Françoise, and told her that whenever they had been together he was in a fever afterwards. She declared her involvement, but was also terrified: after all, he was married and had children. It had all been so sudden. She asked for time to think . . . She would go away for a fortnight to reflect. Mario felt incredibly relieved: Françoise's indecision seemed to him like manna from heaven. All his anxiety melted away as he passionately declared his love, for he knew that a possible unconditional 'yes' from Françoise was thus further postponed. This was the point when Mario telephoned me. After our first meeting, in which he explained the problem to me, we decided to see each other 'as and when we could', with a view to reactivating his self-analysis.

He soon realized that he would not be able to give up his wife and children, and that intense mourning for 'other possible stories' awaited him. With obvious signs of emotion, he described to me the plot of the film *That's Life* (1986), starring Jack Lemmon, which he happened to have seen on television, about the crisis of a man watching himself grow older.

A dream portrayed the danger and the escape from it: he was about to be attacked by a big, violent, impulsive man, but managed to get away from him; then, like a latter-day Ulysses with the Sirens, he also escaped the seduction of a group of women with exaggeratedly pronounced features. He himself thought that the dream had to do with the risk that his narcissistic and characteropathic aspects might be reactivated so as to avoid mourning his wish for a never-ending circular time that constantly rotated about its own axis.

A series of dreams now illustrated this 'struggle' between the attempt at self-assertion by the capacity for mourning and the wish to deny time and give free rein to his narcissism. For instance, in one dream he flung the fountain-pen his father had given him to mark his 'maturity' into the river, while another dream featured a gardener looking after cypresses in a cemetery. Then he dreamed of himself now as a teenager, wearing the clothes he was fond of at that age, and now as a builder 'reconstructing' a building. Next, in one and the same night, he dreamed of himself as a vagrant, a pauper or a gypsy, and as someone looking for keys so that he could go and live in a 'new, comfortable house'. He was gradually realizing the advantages of the new situation – his economic and job security, his children growing up, and the solidity of his affects.

In a dream in which he was walking along country roads, he turned into some unknown streets where there were shops like 'non-return valves': he could only go forward, and it was impossible to turn back. This marked the end of his illusions about the possible circularity of time; from now on he accepted the fact that it flowed in one direction only.

Another dream portrayed an autistic child who was cured; this represented his emergence from the 'ahistorical bubble' in which he had at some point sought refuge, losing contact with reality and with time. There followed a depressive coda with some manic and erotized touches, but he was soon restored to a new, 'reconstructed and satisfying' equilibrium.

Ten years later I saw my engineer again: his life had been happy, his work had been appreciated and his children had married. He told me of the difficulty he and his wife had experienced at being left to live their lives together by themselves again: having almost embarked on the path of conflictual acting out to mask mourning – as in the film *The War of the Roses* (1989) – they had managed to avoid falling into this trap. However, the reason why he had come back to me was to tell me that, on reaching the age of 60, he had had another 'crisis', which had reminded him of the previous one. This time a chat-line had been to blame: he had spent some evenings chatting online with a younger woman, with whom he had become intellectually and emotionally involved, and the relationship had ultimately taken on an increasingly erotic tinge. She too was married, aged about 40, and despite the realization that both he and the 'lady' were seeking an 'erotized' escape from another existential turning point, they had gradually become so involved in the game that they had exchanged email addresses (I was inevitably reminded of the film *You've Got Mail* (1998) and, by association, *Falling in Love* (1984)). They had sent each other long messages and finally exchanged mobile phone numbers.

After deciding to 'meet' one afternoon in a nearby town and to let things take their course, they had agreed at the last moment to 'give up the idea', having become aware of the analgesic, erotized significance of their 'IT-mediated passion'. Mario told me that he had had the following dream: he was on a train, perhaps the only passenger, sitting beside the driver, who was driving the train very calmly and safely; they entered a tunnel full of electrical substations and transformers with very high voltages, and sparks were coming from the posts; there were drops of water (tears?) and sharp bends, but the train continued on its way despite these potential dangers. Although he was worried, the safe driving of the driver calmed him. Then came a precipitous climb; the train seemed to slide, but, with a sure hand, the 'driver' guided it out of the tunnel, mastering the very steep gradient, and finally they emerged into the light. In another dream, he was with a strong, dependable schoolmate, who protected him from an attack by some thugs; his protective friend's strength of character surprised and pleased him.

The force of this second 'pivotal-age crisis' was spent much more quickly: Mario seemed to have taken to heart the crisis of ten years earlier and to have given himself just enough pain-killer and euphoriant to tackle and overcome this fresh onset of depression, to negotiate the violent emotional tensions involved and to come out the other side, knowing that there was a part of himself on which he could totally depend.

He left me with what I saw as a highly significant dream, in terms both of an increased capacity for introspection and of an ability to conceive new plans and expectations. In this dream, he went to Venice, where he entered a cinema to see a film. All of a sudden, someone offered him the chance to witness something hidden and secret – there was a kind of manhole, the entrance to a basement that was the home of some men and women, who were in fact undeveloped, short, stocky 'dwarfs', some of them deformed, some in barrels, and others 'in shit', abandoned in wretchedness and isolation, suffocating and filthy. On an undefined higher level was another 'floor', with masks of noblemen and swordsmen, but they were from the eighteenth century, meaningless and anachronistic. Shaken, he left the cinema and saw a kind of executioner-cum-guard with a hammer and sickle, who was about to go down below, wielding his 'hammer' to prevent the emergence of any cry, the expression of any need or any sign of adversity. The dream 'opened' Mario's eyes to the deep level of needs that had never had a hearing and that he had never realized existed; it showed him the anachronistic quality of the narcissistic choices of the past and created a new possibility of listening to his vital needs, which had been silenced by the terrible superego executioner that had put to death every manifestation of life.

I have had no further news of Mario since, apart from the Christmas cards he sends me every year from France, where he still lives.

Another brief example is the case of a 55-year-old advertising executive who had begun to suffer from depressive and anxious symptoms, which he had attempted unsuccessfully to treat with prescribed drugs. At our first meeting he immediately began to tell me, in great alarm, about the crisis facing his business: he did not know what its future prospects were and was ignorant of its state of 'health'; he agonized about its future all day long and often all night too. I first tried to open up affective pathways so as to enable him to negotiate the emotions bound up with the passage of time now that he had reached the age of 55, and with his changed conception of his role in the family now that his children were growing up. However, all these 'paths' petered out because he denied feeling any emotion in regard to this and other events, instead constantly reverting to his worries about his firm. Only then, prompted also by the 'sound' of his words, did I tell him that he reminded me of Louis XIV's famous remark *L'etat c'est moi!* and that he seemed to be saying to me: 'The business, *c'est moi!*' This struck home like a thunderbolt, and he agreed to a series of meetings with the potential for him to choose psychological treatment. Once this breach had been opened, there emerged a series of *alarms* about the 'time he had left to live', in connection with the ages of his parents and friends when they died, and also about when to retire and what this would involve: either a permanent holiday, or the terrible boredom of 'What do I do next?' after reading the morning paper. Other alarms had to do with loneliness, and little by little possible pathways emerged, which, once narrated, took the place of the depression and anxiety.

The heading of this chapter refers also to pivotal events. This is intended to indicate that, besides crises bound up with changes over time, there are others triggered by 'events' that modify the expected and expectable course of life – 'events' that remain indelibly in memory as a watershed between 'before' and 'after'. They are experienced as catastrophic changes, and entail mourning, readjustment and the achievement of a new equilibrium. An appropriate metaphor from the world of physics might be the ejection of a particle from its orbit. In most cases the events concerned are traumatic and unforeseen, such as a death, accident or serious illness, which totally disrupts all previous equilibria and the subject's accustomed scale of values (F. Guignard, personal communication, 2000). Then comes a period of anguish due to the loss of the previous equilibrium, followed by an often painful phase of readjustment and acquisition of a new *Gestalt*.

That is what happens when things go well. If they do not, a whole series of possibly extreme avoidance measures may be deployed, ranging from different forms of acting out to illness or even suicide. Situations of this kind have been tellingly described by various Argentine authors in the context of analyses conducted under extreme conditions such as military dictatorship (e.g. Puget and Wender 1987). More common examples are devastating bereavements or parents' reactions to serious acute or chronic illness in their children. Acceptance of these situations is often not a simple matter, because the guilt aroused in the subject by the fact of being in good health or still alive complicates the process of working through the emotions activated by the 'change'.

The occasion may be ostensibly trivial. An example is the film mentioned earlier, *The War of the Roses*, in which a couple cannot cope with the new situation arising when their two children leave home to go to college: after some attempts at existential adjustment, they engage in violent conflict with each other – actually a mask for the impossibility of mourning – acting out their characteropathic violence and destruction until they are both dead. Many couples faced with the birth of a severely disabled child respond in a similar way: the weaker partner often leaves the field (and the suffering that pervades it) to embark on another, more gratifying relationship. The onset of a serious illness shatters the entire security system that formerly prevailed, so that previously significant cathexes are devalued and must be replaced by new ones. Old narcissistic wounds are reopened, with the reactivation of experiences of injustice and feelings of guilt and pain in relation to other people.

The working through of such situations is no easy matter. Sometimes it is healthy for it not to be fully accomplished, as in the case of Freud's mourning for his daughter Sophie and for his grandchild; this is unfortunately borne out by many examples from everyday life.

The sense of guilt has to do either with 'things that were not done' or with the realization that one has not been able to protect the person near and dear to one from the blows inflicted by fate. 'Fate' here means the accumulation of chance happenings that ultimately direct the course of life one way or another in a manner beyond the control of the individual.

The difficulty of mourning is skilfully depicted in Dino Buzzati's novella *Larger than Life* (1962), in which a scientist, Professor Endriade, is unable to reconcile himself to the loss of his beloved and builds an enormous machine that reproduces her characteristics. This is reminiscent of Bion's 'no thing', which comes into being when absence cannot be worked through. Another example of the difficulty of mourning can be found in Nanni Moretti's film *The Son's Room* (2001), which narrates the human and emotional vicissitudes of a psychoanalyst who tragically loses a son: finding it impossible to go on working with his patients, he tells them he is giving up work – whether temporarily or permanently we do not know.

I have chosen these two examples at random; as stated, the variations on this theme in every form of artistic expression are infinite.

10

PSYCHOANALYSIS AND NARRATION

In the first session of an analysis, the patient brings a number of bottles of ink, each of which corresponds to a subject to be developed. Some are ready for use as brought; in others, the ink will have 'dried up' and need a diluent contributed by the analyst; while still others contain only residues of ink or are empty: these are the ones it will be most difficult to draw on for the writing of 'lost stories'. The analyst's work will substantially consist in this process of narrative cooperation, into which analyst and patient will dip their narrative nibs so as to develop the condensed inky agglomerate into stories (Ferro 2000d).

In reality, matters are rather more complicated, because what I describe corresponds to the ideal situation of a patient particularly suitable for analysis – i.e., in other words, one who is sufficiently easy for the analyst.

Often the ink is not brought in bottles but squirted on to the analyst, who must work on this 'soaking' with his narrative nib so as to break it down into a story that the patient can assimilate. In other cases the patient may not have any nibs or paper, or the bottles that ought to contain the ink may be flat and two-dimensional – as in Flatland – in which case a whole series of operations, involving the provision of inkwells, pens and paper, must be carried out before the more classical work of writing can be embarked upon (Arrigoni and Barbieri 1998). However, I shall return to these aspects later.

The point I wish to make here is that every analysis calls for a *choice of narrative genre*, which is made in part by the analyst in accordance with his theoretical model. This model may be a reconstruction of the patient's infancy and family romance, a reconnaissance and illumination of the patient's internal world, an emphasis on the characteristics of the relationship arising between analyst and patient, which may be made explicit to a greater or lesser extent, or the creation of a field, or affective theatre, in which all the characters that will eventually populate the analyst's consulting room become three-dimensional, assume bodily form and speak their lines, thus conferring thinkability and expressibility on what had previously been exerting pressure in the form of an 'inexpressible condensate'.

However, the 'narrative genre' is of course chosen and presented by the patient on a daily basis. What matters is the emotion or sequence of emotions the patient wishes to express, or to be helped to express by the analyst. If the emotion is *disorientation, anxiety or loneliness*, this may be expressed in different narrative forms. Here are some examples:

- *A chronicle-type genre*: 'I was at Malpensa Airport when a snowfall put the whole airport out of action and no one knew how to deal with the emergency.' *Or*: 'I saw something on TV that upset me: heavy rain had imprisoned some cavers underground and they could not get out because the cave entrance was blocked by water from a river that had burst its banks. They were left in the dark and cold.'
- *A memory of childhood*: 'I remember once when I was small how my mother was late picking me up from school in the afternoon; it was getting dark and raining and I became more and more frightened.'
- *A sexual genre*: 'I could hardly wait for Monica to come back so we could make love, but she immediately put on her pyjamas and slippers and went to bed with a bad headache.' *Or*: 'While I was making love to Monica, she seemed so remote and cold that I no longer knew who I was with or what I was doing.'
- *A science-fiction genre*: 'I read a book about an extraterrestrial who loses his spaceship and lands on Earth, but has no way of finding his bearings.'

An infinite number of examples could of course be given, but my point is that psychoanalysis is the method that allows emotions to be 'broken down' into narrations, whereby they can be endowed with 'bodily form' and 'visibility'. For me as an analyst, then, what matters is not the individual narration as such, but grasping the emotions that lie upstream of it, the narration being their 'narrative derivative' (in some cases patients must be helped to create a narrative that can convey emotions unknown to them).

But what should we do with patients' narrations? Many schools of psychoanalysis subject (or used to subject) them to interpretation – thus breaking their spell by decoding the patient's words in the form of 'You are telling me that . . .' This is in my view usually harmful, not only because the patient feels humiliated by this 'disconfirmation' of his or her narration, but also, and in particular, because the analyst is merely performing a simultaneous translation into another language (the analyst's own) rather than initiating transformations (Williams 2001). I consider that the best way of bringing about transformations is periodically to grasp the emotions underlying our patients' narration in such a way that they feel that it is understood and shared, thus progressively activating their 'narrative competence'.

The matter is perhaps rather more complicated, because the whole area of the formation of images and the ongoing relationship between these and narrations is also relevant: whereas narrations create images, they are in turn derived from them (Badoni 1997; Bonaminio 1998). Moreover, another function of the analyst is, I believe, to facilitate the creation of affective-climatic coordinates so as to activate the patient's 'imaginopoietic' capacity (Di Benedetto 2000). This can be done by means of an apprenticeship in the analytic laboratory where images are formed from the patient's narration or from what the patient 'leaves unsaid' (Bolognini 1999; Fabbrici 2000; Shon 1997). Image formation (from a wide variety of stimuli) was for a long time seen as the prerogative of dreams (once described as the 'royal road' to the unconscious), but many now consider that a dream-like level of the mind is always active, even if we are unaware of it, and constantly creates images. The main task of psychoanalysis today is to facilitate this process of image formation and to develop the capacity to transcribe the resulting images into narration (Chianese 1997; Demetrio 1995).

Returning to analysis after a long Christmas break, a patient said that he had fallen ill because of the cold and had a prolonged fever. Furthermore, during the holidays a tornado had blown the roof off his house; he had money troubles; and oxygen masks had been deployed on his return flight because the plane's pressurization system had broken down. It would have been easy to interpret all this along orthodox lines: the holiday from his analysis had exposed him to the cold; harmful, violent emotions had been activated; and he had come to the analysis without resources (his overdraft) and gasping for lack of oxygen. I abstained from such decoding, recalling that, once when I had given such an interpretation, the patient's dramatic production in the session had featured the terror he had felt when his father drove dangerously, as well as the story of a serial child killer. So I confined myself to receiving and describing the patient's emotions, saying that these holidays had been a rotten period when he had felt bad, at the end of his resources and filled with fear and suffering *at what had happened*. He replied as follows (note how the text of the session is generated by patient and analyst together in an ongoing duet):

> But a friend of mine was waiting at the airport to pick me up, and my son settled down immediately when we got home; we met up with our friends again, although my son is still afraid of over-intimate relationships that might lead to sex.

Here again, a decoding type of interpretation would be simple: having experienced my previous interpretation as welcoming and receptive, he had immediately felt at ease in the consulting room, even if he was afraid of getting too close. I kept this interpretation back in the 'analytic kitchen area' and presented it to him in the 'restaurant area', cooked as follows:

> It must have been very nice, after all these mishaps, to find a good friend at the airport, and you must have felt relieved to see friendly faces again and be back where you could feel at ease; it's understandable that your son feels the need to keep at a 'safe distance'.

101

He replied that his son had in fact met a girl who was able to keep at the right distance, and that this had made him want a closer relationship without being afraid. Here again I abstained from decoding, but instead grasped the emotions, thereby opening the way to further narrative transformations.

The analyst thus presents him- or herself as a person capable of listening, understanding, grasping and describing the emotions of the field and as a catalyst of further transformations – on the basis that there is not *an unconscious to be revealed*, but a capacity for thinking to be developed, and that the development of the capacity for thinking allows closer and closer contact with previously non-negotiable areas. In more radical terms, the analyst does not decode the unconscious but brings about a development of the conscious mind and a gradual broadening of the unconscious, in accordance with Bion's conception, mentioned earlier, of psychoanalysis as a probe that broadens the field it is exploring.

Another way in which the analyst 'effects transformations' is through changes of vertex.

A brilliant but extremely cautious young lawyer, who was very wary about communicating and did his best to cool down any emotional contact, told me one day that, while at a congress, the principal of his practice had said to him in a hotel vestibule: 'What have you got in that bag, 600 condoms?' – in a reference to his supposed highly active sex life. I commented that there were other possible ways of seeing this text: for example, it might refer to someone who was so cautious and fearful in his 'relations' that he wanted to protect himself not with one but with all of 600 condoms. The patient burst out laughing; a warmer and more affectionate climate arose and he was able to gain access to more intimate matters than those from which he had previously protected himself with – precisely – the 600 condoms.

Another characteristic of the analytic encounter is the polysemy of narrations.

A male patient brought a dream featuring the analyst's consulting room, which contained not only himself and the analyst but also his baby, who was a few months old, an affectionate female colleague and someone who talked too much, thereby robbing him of precious minutes of his analysis. Finally the roof seemed to open up, admitting a blinding light, and a wall of the room fell down, revealing a scene of places from his childhood. I recalled the previous session, in which intimate and delicate subjects had arisen, but in which I had given some long interpretations (talked too much) and had also brought up certain matters in a way the patient had found sudden and disconcerting. He commented on the first part of the dream without adding anything significant, but dwelt on the second part, where something sudden and beyond my control had happened, disconcerting him even if there was no danger, because he had the builders in at his office. I drew the patient's attention to how the consulting room was becoming populated with various characters – tender presences like the baby; affectionate presences like the female colleague; and antipathetic ones like the person who talked too much. Finally, I said that the last scene of the dream seemed to me to be half-way between an earthquake, causing the ceiling to cave in and a wall to fall down, and the words of an old song, 'Heaven in a room', of which I remembered the line 'The room has no walls any more'. So the dream referred to feelings of fear, as well as to entering into something new and the opening up of unexpected scenes. The patient continued to 'populate' and bring to life the infantile scene that had opened up.

In my kitchen, I was of course thinking of the complex effect of some of my remarks of the previous day – a disconcerting effect that, while arousing fear, had also accomplished a widening of meaning. I also reflected on how the patient felt his horizons broadening and the scenes of memory being opened up. At the same time I was aware of his fragility, as manifested in the unsettling effect of 'strong' themes on him. However, I was also thinking – from a different vertex – that he had precisely described a difficult and indeed 'seismic' phase in my own emotional life, although I hoped that my 'builders' could repair the damage. Since it was the patient's last session of the week, I could not help feeling that, again from a different vertex, although the earthquake of separation was present, the patient had staged the relevant emotion by introducing a character, Aurelio, who wanted to stay with him for as long as possible and could not understand that he also had other things to do, like being with his wife and children. We worked on 'Aurelio' and 'Aurelio's' need to have someone near him and never be alone, and the patient added a further link to the narrative chain when he said that, as a little boy, he too had behaved like Aurelio with his mother.

The place of the transference in this conception

'Patients' often make object choices that could be termed 'traumatophilic' because they repeat earlier traumatic patterns of relationship, partly in the hope of dealing with the former 'disastrous' situation with more suitable means than those available at the time (that is, in general, in earliest infancy). In essence, an unsolved problem is being re-presented, in the hope that 'mathematics' will now be available to render it less toxic. This 'repetition of the trauma', which must also come to inhabit the analyst's consulting room, constitutes one of the *historical roots* of psychoanalysis, which drew attention from the beginning to the fundamental importance of infantile experiences. Some patients go on narrating the elements of this drama throughout their lives by bringing about mishaps and choosing links that constantly re-confer form and substance on the trauma. The traumatic infantile experience becomes the organizer of the whole of mental life and indeed the organizer and director of life itself. Analysis eventually becomes the place where the primal traumatic scenes can be reconstructed 'emotional piece by emotional piece' and where, provided that analyst, patient and setting hold, the primal scenario can be transformed.

The childhood of one of my patients had been characterized by parental abandonments, betrayals and deceptions. After a few fruitful years of analysis, we imperceptibly reached an impasse, which in fact turned out to be only apparent: the patient had for years been collecting fragments of information about the analyst's life, behaviour and publications, and had finally been able to construct a scene in which he had proof that the analyst had betrayed him, proof of the analyst's total unreliability, and proof that he did not care at all about his patient. At this crucial juncture the analysis could have become bogged down and discontinued, but the crisis actually proved to be a turning point, allowing the dismantling and transformation of the primal experience, which had come from *there* (the history) to *here*, the only place where it could be modified (perhaps to return, at least in part, to *there* so as to re-inhabit a modified infantile history).

My conception of infantile trauma

By 'infantile trauma' I mean the narrative *Gestalt* assumed by a given patient's aggregate traumatic experiences. A traumatic experience may of course be on the macroscale, but is more often a synergetic accumulation of repeated traumatic microexperiences. These cumulative traumatic microexperiences lead to the symptom, which may also take the form of a dysfunction of the capacity to think or to experience emotions. The problem is always a matter of the proportion or disproportion between the quantities of sense data and proto-emotions to which an experience gives rise and the capacity or incapacity of the instruments available for transforming the 'inputs' received into 'thinkable' experiences. What is not thinkable is either evacuated or encysted pending thinkability.

My conception of infantile sexuality

This is another of the 'historical roots' of psychoanalysis, which, in the early days, was understood in the strict sense of a child's physical sexuality. In my view, infantile sexuality can still be seen as one of the foundations of psychoanalysis (Widlöcher 2000), but with the broader connotation of a sexuality between minds, so that it becomes a way of relating. There is no form of relating that does not involve a coupling of minds, if only because projective identifications are a basic mode of communication. A 'sexual' dysfunction between minds may be narrated by means of a sexual dialect or scene; however, it can of course also be narrated by other scenarios.

Moreover, relationality is a prerequisite for the initiation of mental activity at the very beginning of life. The same applies to the narration of adult sexuality, which I see in terms of a scene that tells me about the patient's psychic and relational functioning.

A male patient said he could not bear the sight of the female genitals and 'consequently' could not have sex. He told me how upset he had once been on seeing a naked little girl at the seaside with her 'terrible wound'; then he remembered feeling ill while on a trip to Africa when he learned about certain tribes where the girls lost their virginity by 'sitting astride' camels. The session continued with an account of a colonoscopy he had had with a long probe. He then returned to the subject of the female genitals as a cut, tear or wound.

If academic notions of castration anxiety are set aside, the reason for 'women' appearing as wounded, torn and bleeding becomes plain. It was because a 'split-off' part of himself massacred and wounded them without his knowledge *before* he arrived on the scene, and when he did arrive he could not mate with someone already 'bestridden' by a camel.

An intrapsychic reading would of course focus on the patient's own female aspects, which were constantly 'wounded and torn apart' by uncontainable and violent aspects of himself, which were violent because they had not yet been made 'thinkable'.

However, the situation is no different from that of another patient, who brought the same 'fabula' with a different plot – that is, a different, non-sexual, narrative scenario.

Massimo

Massimo was a parachutist from the special corps whose father had made him join the army because of the 'bad company he was keeping'. He had subsequently taken part in a number of missions in foreign countries where he had witnessed the massacre and slaughter of many people. All of a sudden, panic attacks had begun, accompanied by a fear of sleeping by himself at home; his wife had gone away shortly before and he was afraid she might be deceiving him.

In this case too, it is impossible to overlook the appearance of unknown parts and aspects – the 'bad company' – which were bursting into his mental life again, so that he was afraid of violent acting out. He feared that he might not be able to stop himself engaging in such acts, owing, for instance, to the 'jealousy' he was as yet unable to experience in relation to his wife – this in turn being a repetition of proto-emotions from his infancy that had never been rendered digestible.

However, the same story could be narrated in yet another way.

Anna

Anna, now 15 years old, had, as a little girl, not found a 'place' in her parents' mind; she had contracted one psychosomatic illness after another and had several episodes of anorexia.

She was described by her parents as 'too good and submissive'. Soon after the beginning of her therapy, she brought some dreams. In the first, she was at her grandmother's house, and was supposed to go down to the cellar, which had a door to the garden. She heard noises and thought: 'It's Grandad.' But suddenly she was faced with a 'man with a knife' who wanted to stab her. Kicking his hands, she escaped and telephoned the police. In the second dream she was at home and heard noises coming from the street door lock. She thought it was her mother, but it was actually a thief. She reached for a pistol and the thief said: 'Would you kill a defenceless soul?' She replied: 'You want to kill someone, but I'm going to kill you,' and killed him. But the more she 'killed' him, the more he immediately came back to life. Then her parents came and she slipped away – thinking: 'Now I shall end up in jail.'

Her split-off parts were looming, and could of course be seen as terrors activated by contact with the analyst or as terrifying forms of split-off functioning. However, they always told the same story – that of an infantile sexuality between minds (or of an infantile intrapsychic sexuality) and not that of adult relationality.

Anna now began one of her sessions by saying that she had to eat 'plain food', and, feeling misunderstood by the therapist, she at once brought a dream in which her 'aunt had had a car accident because she had gone through an amber light'. Her irritation was thus kindled immediately, resulting equally immediately in a crash due to the activation of terribly violent emotions at not being understood and received at once. After another of the therapist's interventions, she added: 'I have to be careful what I eat or drink, because tea causes inflammation, oranges cause inflammation, strawberries cause inflammation and bananas cause inflammation.' So any word was liable to inflame sleeping aspects and cause them to flare up into uncontainable emotions.

Isotta

The story of Isotta, a 14 year old who suffered from tics but was otherwise a model girl, is just the same. It was obvious from the outset that the tics were a way of evacuating otherwise unmanageable proto-emotions. Communication was also very difficult until it occurred to the analyst to suggest that they should make a drawing together (A. Bassetti, personal communuication, 2001). So the analyst drew two curved lines and the drawing was continued by Isotta, who entitled it 'Puss Tobi in Boots'. The background consisted of small blue clouds like the scales of a dragon that had been 'cattified' – or rather 'rabbitized', so tamed did Isotta appear. Yet, as she drew, stories began to germinate in association with the drawing. These ranged from very 'trivial' ones to others featuring a mad dog that had eaten a calf and another dog; one of them was about a boy she knew who was seemingly respectable but in reality a delinquent. In this way, each 'dragon scale' (the little blue clouds) became a story instead of being evacuated.

The underlying theme of all these cases is the same: a problem of early relational failures, resulting in an explosive infantile mental sexuality that could be deactivated by various strategies, but could only begin to be transformed when it encountered an available mind.

My conception of interpretation

Every communication by the patient is 'seen' by the analyst on different screens or in different scenarios – c.g. the history (external factors), the internal world (internal objects), relationship (the analyst–patient relationship in the present) or the field that includes and subsumes them all with a high degree of non-saturation (Chianese 1997). Interpretation may of course be directed to, or touch upon, one or more of these scenarios (Micati 1993; Nissim Momigliano 1984; Renik 1998; Robutti 1992; Rossi 1994; Tuckett 1993). Moreover, it is important to listen to what the patient 'says' after an interpretation of ours in terms not only of something from the history or internal world, but also of a real-time comment on our interpretation. So if a patient talks about his father as an established politician, he is talking about a historical fact (or character), a fact (character) from his internal world, a fact (or character) of the relational here and now with the analyst, and a fact (or character) as the vector of something in the field activated in the consulting room. If an interpretation to that patient is followed by a reference to a cowboy firing a gun and then to his father's brilliant speeches, these 'responses' would draw on the above worlds to various degrees.

For analysts, the present world of the field is particularly significant because it is the locus of transformations. When analysts 'interpret', it is important for them to know that they have a wide range of instruments at their disposal. First, there are the absolutely open, non-saturated interventions I call 'Chauncey interpretations' (the reference is of course to Peter Sellers in the film *Being There* (1979)), which I used to describe as 'Goofy interpretations': these point to metaphorical images on which meaning is conferred by the other. Second, analysts may grasp and describe the emotions present in the consulting room. Third, analysts may undertake a process of alphabetization, in which they attempt to help their patients to appropriate an emotional ABC of their own. Fourth, analysts may hope for the appearance of a 'significatum' (a significatum being like the Virgin Mary in that, as a boy analysand once said, you have to wait for her to appear). Finally, analysts may give saturated, explicit interpretations of the transference focusing on the here and now or on their patients' internal world.

A patient once insisted on my going with him when he went shopping, or at least accompanying him down the stairs. It was not easy to get him to see that, in analysis, I could help him to understand and take possession of the things he needed (the shopping) or to see what it meant to go downstairs to a lower level, but that, being analysis, it could not provide a 'concrete, acted-out response to all his requests'. Accepting this view would also entail mourning for everything he did not have as a child and could not now ever have in the way he would have liked to have it at the time.

In the next session he brought a number of dreams. In the first he was on a bus that was supposed to take him to his session, but it remained stationary; in desperation, he then ran for the last bus that could take him to his session. In the second dream, the family's country house was full of rats that fed on people's faces; and in the third he needed to have a pee, but urinated outside the block of flats because the lavatory door was locked. These dreams enabled me to show him not only that he was aware that the analysis would be stationary like his bus unless he was prepared to change his view of what it could give him, but also that he was worried that he might miss the opportunity for analysis. I was also able to show him how he was constantly gnawing – like the rats – at what he had not had and what the analysis could not give him in concrete form, and that this gnawing was sterile. Finally, I was able to show him how he kept his own needs in check, imagining that the door of my availability would be locked.

These saturated, unequivocal interpretations of his dreams got the analysis going again. I say this in order to point out that there are some situations in which the analyst must interpret actively, precisely and also unequivocally. However, the psychoanalyst's art lies precisely in regulation of the 'breathing' of the analytic field – from non-saturation (inhalation), which expands the field, to saturation (exhalation), which collapses it in an interpretive choice. The analyst in effect acts as a respiratory centre that must constantly modulate the breathing of the field as required.

External reality

A recurring question that arises in connection with the 'field' and the 'characters' (including non-anthropomorphic ones) of the session concerns the attitude to be adopted when patients talk about an element of *objective* reality that they could not possibly leave unmentioned – for instance, a *tumour*. In such a case, of course, one is bound to accept the manifest content of the patient's report and make contact with the pain, terror and shock occasioned by the entry of the 'tumour' into the consulting room. At the same time – provided that the analysis continues and that the triad of patient, analyst and setting remains in existence – I am sure that the 'psychoanalytic imp' would lead me to deconstruct the tumour from its status as an element of external reality and to try to understand it from the point of view of a character in the setting, in terms of an affective hologram (Ferro 1996d, 1996e) of what is being talked about. This of course applies as long as a psychoanalytic setting can be meaningfully upheld.

Giovanna

Following a period of productive work with Giovanna, a prolonged 'lethargy' set in again, with a return of the boredom that seemed to freeze everything. However, I managed to understand how she created the blanket that sent me to sleep: she presented her narration in an absolute monotone, linking everything with coordinating conjunctions – 'and . . . and . . . and . . .' – without any division into main and subordinate clauses to help differentiate and distinguish important communications from secondary ones. Any possible difference was masked by the accumulation of coordinating conjunction upon coordinating conjunction, each seemingly having the same syntactic value. This was so both within individual sessions and from session to session. In this sea, I lost my bearings and almost fell asleep, cradled by all these identical waves.

Any attempt on my part to interpret, or at least describe, what happened after the subject of 'emotions' had arisen proved totally futile until a terrible event burst upon us: 'My family doctor found a swelling on my neck and asked for some tests to be carried out. A few days later I heard that I had a malignant tumour.' The resulting storm stirred that uniform, calm sea into a fury, with the beginning of the prolonged ordeal of tests and, finally, a decision that *urgent surgical intervention* was necessary.

Given the dramatic urgency of these communications, I was bound to take account *also* of their meaning in external reality, but at the same time I increasingly felt the need to find a meaning in terms of what was happening inside the consulting room.

The patient said it might be necessary to remove a '*lobe*' of her thyroid. She added that it was quite impossible for her to discuss this with her *mother* because she was afraid she would be unable to handle it. She also said that the doctors did not yet know whether the tumour was papillary or *follicular*. At this point I too felt compelled to undertake an *urgent intervention*, and told the patient that I had been wondering for some time what she had in her throat that was unable to come out – something she feared might be highly malignant and perhaps mad,* which she was afraid to tell me about in case I could not handle it. Giovanna seemed to hold her breath, but after a while told me in a terrified voice that there was indeed something she had not dared to tell me about in all her years of analysis – something that was in fact the real reason why she had asked for analysis, although she had always thought she would never, ever dare to talk to me about it. She was terrified at the idea that she might be mad, and indeed, what she saw was undeniable: her house was inhabited by ghosts. This led to a living narration that enabled us to subject the 'tumour' to chemotherapy in the consulting room too.

Eventually she asked me whether she was suffering from hallucinations. I told her that they seemed to me more like daydreams, which surely had every right to exist. In this way, session by session, I found myself discovering this world of ghosts, moving fearfully in a space that I felt at times to be one of outright delusion, but which on other occasions seemed more like a play space containing the rudiments of a shareable meaning. I was

---

★ Translator's note: the Italian word for 'mad' is *folle*, which is contained in *follicular*.

saved – on the level of technique too – when I recalled Eduardo de Filippo's play *Ghosts – Italian Style*, which portrays the interaction of the hero with presences in his house that he quite naturally sees as ghosts with whom he forms meaningful relationships.

The patient now underwent surgery in a cancer ward. When the biopsy confirmed that the tumour was not follicular but papillary, the patient was relieved, and commented that, whereas the former was very serious and a 'cold' nodule, the latter was a 'warm' nodule. In this way we gained access to the subject of the passions. As the patient explained, 'the boredom was a way of jumping over the coals lit up by the passions', and the ghosts now also indicated passion and warmth, albeit encysted, rather than cold paranoia. I must confess to having been afraid that fiery passions might be stoked up while the ghostly fabric was still in the process of being woven.

Metabolization of the ghosts and entry into their realm triggered the miracle: the boredom disappeared, and with it the sleepiness. Intense and even violent emotions were kindled, all of them with the theme of 'not having a place for herself'. This was due to the patient's infantile history: although several rooms were available, she had not been given one of her own, but instead assigned a temporary, movable place in the living room (she likewise experienced the couch as precarious and not stably her own). Moreover, her preoccupied mother had had space only for her own hypochondriacal anxieties and not for her daughter's anxieties, worries or plans. Giovanna reacted very violently whenever a session had to be cancelled; for her, this was tangible proof that there was no place for her, and she always responded with episodes of fury and despair.

One element in this reawakening was a reverie of mine that ensued from her comment: 'I feel as if there is a *rubber wall* that I can beat against, but no one answers', which put me in mind of the padded cells in old-fashioned psychiatric wards. When I told her this, she was shocked and deeply moved. Emotions, it appeared, could only be put to sleep or contained in a room intended for raving lunatics.

Another dream featured frightening Zulus, but the primitive emotions were no longer put to sleep and there was no longer a rubber wall: the emotions could emerge, even if they inspired fear. After a cancelled session, she dreamed that the keys to her house were broken, so that she could not return; this dream was accompanied by an unprecedented – 'black' – anxiety. 'Black as the Zulus,' I said.

In all my years as an analyst, I have in fact never received an 'external-reality' communication that, when considered from a certain vertex, did not have an important meaning for the relevant analysis. Whether this meaning should be interpreted to the patient or should remain in the analyst's mind until it can be communicated constructively to the patient is another matter.

The place to be assigned to classical concepts

I have also been asked what place there is in a model based on the notions of narratology, transformation and the field for concepts such as resistances, defences, internal objects or unconscious fantasies, and, more specifically, whether the egos of analyst and patient remain distinct in the field. It must, I think, be accepted that this kind of language, relevant and central as it is to other models, becomes less meaningful in my customary approach, in which other concepts are more significant. I do of course believe that every analyst must also be familiar with, and know how to negotiate, other psychoanalytic languages – both for reasons of his essential inner freedom and to facilitate understanding, exchanges and hence enrichment with colleagues who use other models. Again, I regard concepts and structures as instruments with a provisional value, useful for stimulating thought, rather than as entities with value in themselves – which can easily become 'idols' (Britton 2001) that block the development of thought.

My approach therefore concentrates on the promotion of transformation by narrations and the way in which this process takes place.

Bibliography

Abbott, E. (1899) *Flatland: A Romance of Many Dimensions*, Boston, Mass.: Little, Brown.

Ambrosiano, L. (1997) 'Cristallizzazione, dissolvenza e trasformazioni, in Emozioni e interpretazione', E. Gaburri (ed.), Turin: Bollati Boringhieri.

Andrade de Azevedo, A.M. (1996) 'Interpretation: revelation or creation?', paper presented at the symposium *Bion in São Paulo: Resonances*, São Paulo, 14 November.

Arrigoni, M.R., and Barbieri, G.L. (1998) *Narrazione e psicoanalisi*, Milan: Raffaello Cortina.

Badoni, M. (1997) 'Intreccio di immagini e costruzioni: l'ambiente di cura', *Quaderni di Psicoterapia Infantile*, 36: 47–61.

Barale, F., and Ferro, A. (1992) 'Negative therapeutic reactions and microfractures in analytic communication', in *Shared Experience: the Psychoanalytic Dialogue*, L. Nissim Momigliano and A. Robutti (eds), London: Karnac.

Baranger, M., and Baranger, W. (1961–62) 'La situación analítica como campo dinámico', *Revista Uruguaya de Psicoanálisis*, 4: 3–54.

—— (1964) 'Insight in the analytic situation', in *Psychoanalysis in the Americas*, R.E. Litman (ed.), New York: International Universities Press, 1966.

—— (1969) *Problemas del campo psicoanalítico*, Buenos Aires: Kargieman.

Baruzzi, A. (1998) 'Prefazione', in *Memoria del futuro* [Italian translation of Bion 1975], Milan: Raffaello Cortina.

Bezoari, M., and Ferro, A. (1990a) 'Elementos de un modelo del campo analítico: los agregados funcionales', *Revista de Psicoanálisis*, 5/6: 847–861.

—— (1990b) 'Parole, immagini, affetti. L'avventura del senso nell'incontro analitico', in *In due dietro il lettino. Scritti in onore di Luciana Nissim Momigliano*, G. Bartoli (ed.), Castrovillari: Teda Edizioni.

—— (1991a) 'L'oscillazione significati-affetti', *Rivista di Psicoanalisi*, 38: 380–403.

—— (1991b) 'From a play between "parts" to transformations in the couple. Psychoanalysis in a bipersonal field', in *Shared Experience: the Psychoanalytic Dialogue*, L. Nissim Momigliano and A. Robutti (eds), London: Karnac, 1992.

—— (1992) 'I personaggi della seduta come aggregati funzionali del campo analitico', *Notiziario SPI*, Supplemento 2: 103–115, Rome: Borla.

—— (1994a) 'Il posto del sogno all'interno di una teoria del campo analitico', *Rivista di Psicoanalisi*, 40: 251–272.

—— (1994b) 'Listening, interpreting, and psychic change in the analytic dialogue', *International Forum of Psychoanalysis*, 3: 35–41.

—— (1999) 'The dream within a field theory: functional aggregates and narrations', *Journal of Melanie Klein and Object Relations*, 17: 333–348.

Bianchedi, E.T. (1995) 'Creative writers and dream-work-alpha', in *On Freud's Creative Writers and Day-Dreaming*, London: Yale University Press.

Bion, W.R. (1962) *Learning from Experience*, London: Heinemann.

—— (1963) *Elements of Psycho-Analysis*, London: Heinemann.

—— (1965) *Transformations*, London: Heinemann.

—— (1966) 'Catastrophic change', *Bulletin of the British Psycho-Analytical Society*, no. 5.

—— (1970) *Attention and Interpretation*, London: Tavistock.

—— (1973) *Bion's Brazilian Lectures 1*, in *Clinical Seminars and Four Papers*, F. Bion (ed.), Abingdon: Fleetwood Press, 1987.

—— (1974) *Bion's Brazilian Lectures 2*, in *Clinical Seminars and Four Papers*, F. Bion (ed.), Abingdon: Fleetwood Press, 1987.

—— (1975) *A Memoir of the Future, Book 1, The Dream*, Rio de Janeiro: Imago.

—— (1976) 'Evidence', in *Clinical Seminars and Four Papers*, F. Bion (ed.), Abingdon: Fleetwood Press, 1987.

—— (1977) 'On a quotation from Freud', in *Clinical Seminars and Four Papers*, F. Bion (ed.), Abingdon: Fleetwood Press, 1987.

—— (1979a) 'Making the best of a bad job', in *Clinical Seminars and Four Papers*, F. Bion (ed.), Abingdon: Fleetwood Press, 1987.

—— (1979b) *A Memoir of the Future, Book 3, The Dawn of Oblivion*, Rio de Janeiro: Imago Editora.

—— (1980) *Bion in New York and São Paulo*, F. Bion (ed.), London: Karnac.

—— (1985) *Seminari italiani*, F. Bion (ed.), Rome: Borla.

—— (1987) *Clinical Seminars and Four Papers*, F. Bion (ed.), Abingdon: Fleetwood Press.

—— (1992) *Cogitations*, F. Bion (ed.), London: Karnac.

Bion Talamo, P. (1987) 'Perchè non possiamo dirci bioniani', *Gruppo e funzione analitica*, 8: 279–284.

Blixen, K. (1937) *Out of Africa*, London: Putnam.

Bolognini, S. (1997) 'Empatia e patologie gravi', in *Quale psicoanalisi per le psicosi?*, A. Correale and R. Rinaldi (eds), Milan: Raffaello Cortina.

—— (1999) *Come vento come onda*, Turin: Bollati Boringhieri.

Bonaminio, V. (1993) 'Del non interpretare', *Rivista di Psicoanalisi*, 39: 453–477.

—— (1998) 'Spazio analitico e spazio onirico individuale attraverso un frammento clinico', *Rivista di Psicoanalisi*, 44: 129–145.

Borgogno, F. (1999) *La Psicoanalisi come percorso*, Turin: Bollati Boringhieri.

Britton, R. (2001) 'Deification of person or process: idolatry and fundamentalism in psychoanalytic practice', *Bulletin of the European Psychoanalytical Federation*, 55: 65–78.

Buzzati, D. (1962) *Larger than Life [Il grande ritratto]*, trans. H. Reed, London: Secker & Warburg.

Calvino I. (1973) *The Castle of Crossed Destinies*, trans. W. Weaver, London: Vintage, 1977.

Cancrini, T., and Giordo, G. (1995) *Una nave nella tempesta, le bottiglie nel mare: funzioni comunicative e creative del disegno infantile nel rapporto analitico*, II Colloquio nazionale analisi infantile, Milan.

Chianese, D. (1997) *Costruzioni e campo analitico*, Rome: Borla.

Corrao, F. (1981) 'Il modello trasformazionale del pensiero', *Rivista di Psicoanalisi*, 27: 673–683.

—— (1991) 'Trasformazioni narrative', in *Orme*, vol. 1, Milan: Raffaello Cortina, 1998.

—— (1992) *Modelli psicoanalitici: mito, passione, memoria*, Rome: Laterza.

Corrente, G. (1992) 'Trasformazioni del campo ↔ identità', *Gruppo e Funzione Analitica*, 13: 67–72.

De León de Bernardi, B. (1988) 'Interpretación, acercamiento analítico y creatividad', *Revista Uruguaya de Psicoanálisis*, 68: 57–68.

Demetrio, D. (1995) *Raccontarsi*, Milan: Raffaello Cortina.

Di Benedetto A. (2000) *Prima della parola*, Milan: Franco Angeli.

Di Chiara, G. (1985) 'Una prospettiva psicoanalitica del dopo Freud: un posto per l'altro', *Rivista di Psicoanalisi*, 31: 451–461.

—— (1992) 'Meeting, telling, parting: three basic factors in the psychoanalytic experience', in *Shared Experience: the Psychoanalytic Dialogue*, L. Nissim Momigliano and A. Robutti (eds), London: Karnac.

—— (1997) 'La formazione e le evoluzioni del campo psicoanalitico', in *Emozione e interpretazione*, E. Gaburri (ed.), Turin: Bollati Boringhieri.

Duparc, F. (1998) *L'Elaboration*, Paris: L'Esprit du temps.

Eco, U. (1979) *Lector in fabula*, Milan: Bompiani.

—— (1990) *The Limits of Interpretation*, Bloomington, Ind.: Indiana University Press.

Eizirik, C.L. (1996) 'Panel report: psychic reality and clinical technique', *International Journal of Psycho-Analysis*, 77: 37–41.

Fabbrici, C. (2000) *Nel caravanserraglio*, Rome: Borla.

Faimberg, H. (1988) 'A l'écoute du télescopage des générations: pertinence psychanalytique du concept', *Topique*, 42: 223–228.

—— (1989) 'Sans mémoire et sans désir: à qui s'adressait Bion', *Revue Française de Psychanalyse*, 53: 1453–1461.

—— (1996) 'Listening to listening', *International Journal of Psycho-Analysis*, 77: 667–677.

Ferrandino, G. (1993) *Pericle il nero*, London: Granta.

Ferro, A. (1987) 'Il mondo alla rovescia. L'inversione del flusso delle identificazioni proiettive', *Rivista di Psicoanalisi*, 33: 59–77.

—— (1991a) 'From Raging Bull to Theseus: the long path of a transformation', *International Journal of Psycho-Analysis*, 72: 417–425.

—— (1991b) 'La mente del analista en su trabajo: problemas, riesgos, necesidades', *Revista de Psicoanálisis*, 5/6: 1159–1177.

—— (1992) *The Bipersonal Field: Experiences in Child Analysis*, London: Routledge, 1999.

—— (1993a) 'Disegno, identificazione proiettiva e processi trasformativi', *Rivista di Psicoanalisi*, 39: 667–680.

—— (1993b) 'From hallucination to dream: from evacuation to the tolerability of pain in the analysis of a preadolescent', *Psychoanalytic Review*, 80: 389–404.

—— (1993c) 'The impasse within a theory of the analytic field: possible vertices of observation', *International Journal of Psycho-Analysis*, 74: 917–929.

—— (1994a) 'Criterios sobre la analizabilidad y el final del análisis dentro de una teoría del campo', *Revista de Psicoanálisis*, 51: 97–114.

—— (1994b) 'Del campo e dei suoi eventi', *Quaderni di Psicoterapia Infantile*, 30: 39–52.

—— (1994c) 'El diálogo analítico: mundos posibles y transformaciones en el campo analítico', *Revista de Psicoanálisis*, 51: 771–790.

—— (1994d) 'Gruppalità interne di relazione e di campo nell'analisi duale', *Gruppo e Funzione Analitica*, Quaderni, 1, Rome: Borla.

—— (1994e) 'Il dialogo analitico: costituzione e trasformazione di mondi possibili', *Rivista di Psicoanalisi*, 40: 389–409.

—— (1994f) 'Mondi possibili e capacità negative dell'analista al lavoro', Atti X Congresso Nazionale SPI, Rimini.

—— (1994g) 'Two authors in search of characters: the relationship, the field, the story', *Australian Journal of Psychotherapy*, 13: 117–136.

—— (1996a) 'Sexuality as a narrative genre or dialect in the consulting-room: a radical vertex', in *W.R. Bion between Past and Future*, P. Bion Talamo, F. Borgogno and S. Merciai (eds), London: Karnac, 2000.

—— (1996b) 'Carla's panic attacks: insight and transformations: what comes out of the cracks: monster or nascent thoughts?', *International Journal of Psycho-Analysis*, 77: 997–1011.

—— (1996c) 'Elógio da fileira C: a psicanálise como forma particular de literatura', in L.C. Uchôa Junqueira Filho (ed.), *Silêncios e luzes: sobre a experiência psíquica do vazio e da forma*, São Paulo: Casa do Psicólogo.

—— (1996d) '¿Los personajes del cuarto de análisis: qué realidad?', *Revista de Psicoanálisis de Madrid*, 23: 133–142.

—— (1996e) *In the Analyst's Consulting Room*, trans. P. Slotkin, Hove: Brunner-Routledge, 2002.

—— (1997) 'La mente dell'analista tra capacità negative e fatto prescelto: la costruzione di storie', in *Il campo gruppale*, G. Rugi and E. Gaburri (eds), Rome: Borla.

—— (1998a) 'Il sogno della veglia: teoria e clinica', Relazione al Congresso Nazionale SPI, Rome.

—— (1998b) *Antonino Ferro em São Paulo. Séminarios*, M.O. de A. França and M. Petricciani (eds), São Paulo: Editora Sociedade Brasileira de Psicanálise de São Paulo, Acervo Psicanalítico.

—— (1998c) 'Continente inadequado e violência das emoções: dinossauros e tartarugas', lecture to the São Paulo and Porto Alegre Psychoanalytic Centre, November.

—— (1998d) 'Unity of analysis underlying the similarities and differences in the analysis of children and adolescents', *Bulletin of the European Psychoanalytical Federation*, 50: 48–58.

—— (1999a) *La psicoanalisi come letteratura e terapia*, Milan: Raffaello Cortina.

—— (1999b) ' "Characters" and their precursor in depression: experiences and transformation in the course of therapy', *Journal of Melanie Klein and Object Relations*, 17: 119–133.

—— (1999c) 'Camp terapèutic i transformacions emocionals', *III Jornades del Departament de Psiquiatria i Psicologia*, Barcelona: Fundació Hospital Sant Pere Claver.

—— (1999d) 'Construction d'une histoire, dessin et jeu dans l'analyse d'enfants', *Psychothérapie psychanalytique de l'enfant et de sa famille*, sous la direction de Simone Decobert et François Sacco, ERES, 2000.

—— (1999e) 'Narrative derivatives of alpha elements: clinical implications', presented at the IPA Congress, Santiago de Chile, July. Also in *International Forum of Psychoanalysis*, 11: 184–187, 2002.

—— (1999f) 'Interprétations, déconstructions, récits ou les raisons de Jacques', Colloquio Italo-Francese (SPP-SPI), November 1999, Toulouse.

—— (2000a) 'L'après-coup et la cigogne: champ analytique et pensée onirique', Conference of the Paris Psychoanalytical Society (SPP), May.

—— (2000b) 'O respeito pela mente', *IDE* (Sociedade Brasileira de Psicanálise de São Paulo), 32: 39–40.

—— (2000c) 'Cultura da reverie, cultura da evacuação', opening lecture at the 23rd FEPAL Congress, Gramado (Porto Alegre). Also in *Enfance Psy*, 13: 129–136.

—— (2000d) 'Le jeu: personnages, récits, interprétations', *Journal de la Psychanalyse de l'enfant*, 26: 139–160.

—— (2001a) 'Séparation entre rêve et évacuation', *Revue Française de Psychanalyse*, 65: 489–498.

—— (2001b) 'Rêve de la veille et narration', *Revue Française de Psychanalyse*, 65: 285–297.

—— (2001c) 'Marcella: from an explosive sensoriality to the ability to think', IPA Congress, Nice. Also in *Psychoanalytic Quarterly*, 72: 183–200, 2003.

—— (2003) *O pensamento clínico de Antonino Ferro – Conferências e Seminários*, Rio de Janeiro: Casa do Psicólogo.

Ferro, A., and Meregnani, A. (1994) 'Listening and transformative functions in the psychoanalytical dialogue', *Bulletin of the European Psychoanalytical Federation*, 42: 21–29.

—— (1998) 'The inversion of the flow of projective identification in the analyst at work', *Australian Journal of Psychotherapy*, 16: 94–112.

Ferruta, A., Goisis, P.R., Jaffé, R., and Loiacono, N. (2000) *Il contributo della psicoanalisi nella cura delle patologie gravi in infanzia e adolescenza*, Rome: Armando.

Fonagy, P., and Sandler, A-M. (1995) 'On transference and its interpretation', *Bulletin of the European Psychoanalytical Federation*, 45: 5–26.

Freud, S. (1921) *Group Psychology and the Analysis of the Ego*, in *Standard Edition*, vol. 18, London: Hogarth Press, pp. 69–143.

—— (1923) *The Ego and the Id*, in *Standard Edition*, vol. 19, London: Hogarth Press, pp. 12–59.

—— (1933) *New Introductory Lectures on Psycho-Analysis*, in *Standard Edition*, vol. 22, London: Hogarth Press, pp. 5–182.

Gabbard, G., and Lester, E.P. (1995) *Boundaries and Boundary Violations in Psychoanalysis*, New York: Basic Books.

Gaburri, E. (1982) 'Una ipotesi di relazione tra trasgressione e pensiero', *Rivista di Psicoanalisi*, 28: 511–525.

—— (1986) 'Dal gemello immaginario al compagno segreto', *Rivista di Psicoanalisi*, 32: 509–520.

—— (1987) 'Narrazione e interpretazione', in *Psicoanalisi e narrazione*, E. Morpugo and V. Egidi (eds), Ancona: Il Lavoro Editoriale.

—— (ed.) (1997) *Emozione ed Interpretazione*, Turin: Bollati Boringhieri.

Gaburri, E., and Ferro, A. (1988) 'Gli sviluppi kleiniani e Bion', in *Trattato di psicoanalisi*, A. Semi (ed.), vol. 1, Milan: Raffaello Cortina.

Gibeault, A. (1991) 'Interpretation and transference', *Bulletin of the European Psychoanalytical Federation*, 36: 47–61.

Green, A. (1973) *Le Discours vivant*, Paris: Presses Universitaires de France.

—— (1993) *The Work of the Negative*, trans. A. Weller, London: Free Association, 1999.

—— (1998) Foreword to F. Duparc, *L'Elaboration*, Paris: L'Esprit du temps.

Grinberg, L., and Grinberg, R. (1978) 'Aspetti normali e patologici del Super-Io e dell'Ideale dell'Io', in *Super-Io e Ideale dell'Io*, M. Mancia (ed.), Milan: Il Formichiere, 1979.

Guignard, F. (1996) *Au vif de l'infantile*, Lausanne: Delachaux & Niestlé.

—— (1997) *Epître à l'objet*, Paris: Presses Universitaires de France.

—— (1998) 'The interpretation of oedipal configurations in child analysis', *Bulletin of the European Psychoanalytical Federation*, 50: 33–41.

Harris, T. (1981) *Red Dragon*, New York: Putnam.

—— (1988) *The Silence of the Lambs*, New York: St Martin's Press.

—— (1999) *Hannibal*, New York: Delacorte Press.

Hautmann, G. (1977) 'Pensiero onirico e realtà psichica', *Rivista di Psicoanalisi*, 23: 62–127.

Jacobs, T. (1999) 'On the question of self-disclosure by the analyst: error or advance in technique?', *Psychoanalytic Quarterly*, 63: 159–183.

Jaques, E. (1965) 'Death and the mid-life crisis', *International Journal of Psycho-Analysis*, 46: 502–514.

Kaës, R., Faimberg, H., Enriquez, M., and Baranes, J.J. (1993) *Transmission de la vie psychique entre générations*, Paris: Dunod.

Kancyper, L. (1990) 'Narcisismo y pigmalionismo', *Revista de Psicoanálisis*, 48: 1003–1023.

—— (1997) *La confrontación generacional*, Buenos Aires: Paidós.

Kernberg, O. (1993) 'Convergences and divergences in contemporary psychoanalytic technique', *International Journal of Psycho-Analysis*, 74: 659–673.

—— (1996) 'Interpretação: revelação ou criação?', paper discussed at the symposium *Bion in São Paulo: Resonances*, São Paulo, 14 November.

Klein, M. (1928) *Early Stages of the Oedipus Complex*, in *The Writings of Melanie Klein*, vol. 1, London: Hogarth Press, 1975.

—— (1945) *The Oedipus Complex in the Light of Early Anxiety*, in *The Writings of Melanie Klein*, vol. 1, London: Hogarth Press, 1975.

Lowndes, M.B. (1913) *The Lodger*, London: Methuen.

Lussana, P. (1991) 'Dalla interpretazione kleiniana alla interpretazione bioniana attraverso l'osservazione dell'infante', presented at AIPPI, Rome, 2 June.

Mabilde, L.C. (1993) 'Conceito de relação de objeto em psicanálise', *Revista de Psican-álise de SPPA*, 1: 53–70.

Mancia, M., and Meltzer, D. (1981) 'Ego ideal functions and the psychoanalytic process', *International Journal of Psycho-Analysis*, 62: 243–250.

Manfredi, S. (1979) 'Super-Io e Ideale dell'Io come funzioni degli oggetti interni', in *Super-Io e Ideale dell'Io*, M. Mancia (ed.), Milan: Il Formichiere.

Meltzer, D. (1967) *The Psycho-Analytical Process*, London: Heinemann.

—— (1973) *Sexual States of Mind*, Perthshire: Clunie Press.

—— (1992) *The Claustrum: An Investigation of Claustrophobia*, Perthshire: Clunie Press.

Micati, L. (1993) 'Quanta realtà può essere tollerata?', *Rivista di Psicoanalisi*, 39: 153–163.

Nissim Momigliano, L. (1979) 'Come si originano le interpretazioni dell'analista', *Rivista di Psicoanalisi*, 20: 144–175.

—— (1984) 'Due persone che parlano in una stanza', *Rivista di Psicoanalisi*, 30: 1–17.

Norman, J. (2001) 'The psychoanalyst and the baby: a new look at work with infants', *International Journal of Psycho-Analysis*, 82: 83–100.

Ogden, T. (1979) 'On projective identification', *International Journal of Psycho-Analysis*, 60: 357–373.

—— (1997) *Reverie and Interpretation*, Northvale, NJ: Jason Aronson.

—— (2001) *Conversations at the Frontier of Dreaming*, Northvale, NJ: Jason Aronson.

O'Shaughnessy, E. (1999) 'Relating to the superego', *International Journal of Psycho-Analysis*, 80: 861–870.

Puget, J., and Wender, S. (1987) 'Aux limites de l'analysabilité. Tyrannie corporelle et sociale', *Revue Française de Psychanalyse*, 51: 869–885.

Quinodoz, J-M. (2001) *Dreams that Turn Over a Page*, trans. P. Slotkin, Hove: Brunner-Routledge, 2002.

Rella, F. (1999) *Pensare per figure: Freud, Platone, Kafka*, Bologna: Pendragon.

Renik, O. (1993). 'Countertransference enactment and the psychoanalytic process', in *Psychic Structure and Psychic Change: Essays in Honor of Robert S. Wallerstein, M.D.*, M.J. Horowitz, O.F. Kernberg and E.M. Weinshel (eds), Madison, Conn.: International Universities Press.

—— (1998) 'The analyst's subjectivity and the analyst's objectivity', *International Journal of Psycho-Analysis*, 79: 487–498.

—— (1999) 'Playing one's cards face up in analysis: an approach to the problem of self-disclosure', *Psychoanalytic Quarterly*, 68: 521–539.

Ribeiro de Moraes, M.M. (1999) 'Hostile and benign reverie', *Journal of Melanie Klein and Object Relations*, 17: 161–180.

Riolo, F. (1989) 'Teoria delle trasformazioni. Tre seminari su Bion', *Gruppo e funzione analitica*, 10: 7–41.

Robutti, A. (1992) 'Introduction', in *Shared Experience: the Psychoanalytic Dialogue*, L. Nissim Momigliano and A. Robutti (eds), London: Karnac.

Rocha Barros, E. (1994) 'A interpretação: seus pressupostos teóricos', *Revista de Psicanálise SPPA*, 1: 57–72.

—— (2000) 'Affect and pictographic image: the constitution of meaning in mental life', *International Journal of Psycho-Analysis*, 81: 1087–1099.

Rossi, P.L. (1994) 'Attività e passività dell'analista negli inizi difficili in psicoanalisi', Atti del X Congresso SPI, Rimini.

Sarno, L. (1994) 'Transfert, controtransfert e campo psicoanalitico', Atti del X Congresso SPI, Rimini.

Shon, A. (1997) *Vuol dire*, Turin: Bollati Boringhieri.

Smith, H. (1999) 'Subjectivity and objectivity in analytic listening', *Journal of the American Psychoanalytic Association*, 47: 465–484.

Speziale Bagliacca, R. (1998) *Guilt: Reflections on Remorse, Revenge and Responsibility*, Hove: Brunner-Routledge, 2004.

Tuckett, D. (1993) 'Some thoughts on the presentation and discussion of the clinical material of psychoanalysis', *International Journal of Psycho-Analysis*, 74: 1175–1189.

Vallino Macciò, D. (1998) *Raccontami una storia*, Rome: Borla.

Widlöcher, D. (1978) 'The ego ideal of the psychoanalyst', *International Journal of Psycho-Analysis*, 59: 387–390.

—— (2000) 'El lugar de la sexualidad infantil en la cultura contemporánea', presented at the FEPAL Congress, Gramado.

119

Williams, P. (2001) 'Some difficulties in the analysis of a withdrawn patient', *International Journal of Psycho-Analysis*, 82: 727–746.

Winnicott, D. (1947) 'Hate in the countertransference', *International Journal of Psycho-Analysis*, 30: 69–74.

—— (1958) 'The capacity to be alone', in *The Maturational Processes and the Facilitating Environment*, London: Hogarth Press, 1965.

—— (1971) *Therapeutic Consultations in Child Psychiatry*, London: Hogarth Press.

—— (1974) 'Fear of breakdown', *International Review of Psychoanalysis*, 1: 103–107.

Index